101 ways to develop your people, without really trying!

Peter Honey

British Library Cataloguing in Publication Data
A catalogue record for this book is available from the British Library

ISBN 0 9508444 9 7

Published by Dr Peter Honey, Ardingly House, 10 Linden Avenue, Maidenhead, Berkshire SL6 6HB.
Telephone 01628 33946 Fax 01628 33262.

Contents

Acknowledgements

To my family for tolerating me while I worked on another book

To Suzanne Hill for working with me on another book (and tolerating me too!)

To Alan Hurst for the cartoons

To my colleagues on the design team of Ford Motor Company's Supervisory Skills Program who contributed to the attitudes questionnaire (see the introduction).

Preface

Developing people has long been held to be one of the most important responsibilities of any manager. Yet few managers regard themselves as developers either because they see it as an unwelcome distraction from their 'proper' work or because they feel unsure how to go about it.

Predictably, this book is written to help managers

- accept that developing people is proper work - arguably the most proper work of all

- see how developing people, far from being a distraction, adds value to whatever has to be achieved

- know what to do in the normal course of events to provide people with development opportunities.

This book rests on just three basic assumptions

- that a manager, by definition, has a bigger job than he or she can accomplish single handed and therefore has at least two helpers (unfortunately, usually referred to as subordinates)

- that learning and development are for all practical purposes synonymous. Help people learn and they develop. Help people develop and they learn

- that people learn all the time and that everything that happens has an impact, for better or worse, on their learning and development.

If you scan the contents page of this book and think 'there's nothing new here' — that's *good*! The whole idea is to show how to use perfectly ordinary everyday experiences as learning opportunities.

Peter Honey
October 1994

Introduction: Attitudes about developing people

Some managers continually provide their subordinates with opportunities to develop and make it a priority to do so. Other managers assume they are primarily in business to achieve results and have developing people as a secondary goal.

To establish how easy or difficult you will find it to accept the need to help people develop, run down the following statements ticking the ones you agree with and crossing the ones you disagree with. Please respond to each statement with either a tick or a cross however marginal the difference. Be honest with yourself!

1 ☐ People who are busy doing their job, learn and develop automatically.

2 ☐ Developing people is an on-going process, not a single event.

3 ☐ The prime purpose of development is to lift the performance of poor performers.

4 ☐ Development is best done off-the-job, eg on courses, conferences, seminars and workshops.

5 ☐ In general people learn and develop when they need to or have to, ie when they have no choice.

6 ☐ Creating developmental opportunities is a prime responsibility of any manager.

7 ☐ Some people are incapable of further development.

8 ☐ Most people respond best to praise and recognition.

9 ☐ The best way to develop people is to let them have a go and learn from their mistakes.

10 ☐ It is up to managers alone to assess the strengths and development needs of their subordinates.

11 ☐ Development is best done in the work place.

12 ☐ Developing people inevitably raises false hopes and expectations of promotion.

13 ☐ It is just as important to learn from successes as it is to learn from mistakes.

14 ☐ No matter how expert someone is, there is always room for improvement.

15 ☐ Most people respond best to criticism and/or the threat of unpleasant consequences if their performance is unsatisfactory.

16 ☐ Managers cannot *make* people develop - only make it more likely that they will.

17 ☐ The best way to develop people is to set them a challenge on a 'sink or swim' basis.

18 ☐ The prime purpose of development is to help everyone continuously to improve their performance.

19 ☐ Some jobs are so routine and prescribed that they offer no learning opportunities.

20 ☐ Ultimately everyone has to take responsibility for their own development, ie all development is self-development.

Ten of the above statements describe attitudes that will help you accept the need to develop your people and ten describe attitudes that hinder. To establish which you subscribe to move your ticks and crosses into the boxes below

1	□	2	□
3	□	5	□
4	□	6	□
7	□	8	□
9	□	11	□
10	□	13	□
12	□	14	□
15	□	16	□
17	□	18	□
19	□	20	□

□ 　　　　　　　　　　□

Attitudes that
hinder
development

Attitudes that
help
development

If you are a paragon of virtue you will have ten crosses in the left hand column and ten ticks in the right hand column. Any ticks on the left and crosses on the right alert you to attitudes that need to be overhauled. Here are short commentaries on each of the attitudes included in the checklist. It is not necessary to read them all; only the ones where you finished up with ticks on the left or crosses on the right of the key.

1. **People who are busy doing their job, learn and develop automatically. (Approved answer, no.)**

   If you ticked this, in a sense you are quite right. Lots of work based learning is 'automatic' or subliminal. However, believing this means that you are likely to assume that keeping people busy is a sufficient condition for learning and development to occur. Beware. It is just as easy for people, when left to their own devices, to learn the *wrong* things. Learning and development are welcome spin-offs from work but it is rarely safe to assume either the quantity or quality of what is learned.

2. **Developing people is an on-going process, not a single event. (Approved answer, yes.)**

   Many managers find it a rather depressing thought, but development is always continuous and never-ending. There may be specific *events* that contribute to someone's development, but it never really makes sense to say 'been there, done that'. There is *always* something else to learn.

3. **The prime purpose of development is to lift the performance of poor performers. (Approved answer, no.)**

   The prime purpose of development is to help *everyone* continuously to improve their performance (look ahead and see if you ticked item 18.) Development is for all; poor, satisfactory, and brilliant performers. No-one is immune. No-one is exempt.

4. **Development is best done off-the-job, eg on courses, conferences, seminars and workshops. (Approved answer, no.)**

   Clearly, off-the-job learning opportunities have a contribution to make but it is a mistake to believe that they are 'best'. The case for work-based development is a strong one simply because people spend far more time doing their job than attending courses or conferences. The trick is to get work and development to go hand in hand as parallel, totally complimentary activities.

5. **In general people learn and develop when they need to or have to, ie when they have no choice. (Approved answer, yes.)**

Necessity is not only the mother of invention but of learning too. If you offer learning and development on a 'take it or leave it' discretionary basis, most people simply won't get round to it (or assume it happens automatically as in item 1 above). Whilst in the final analysis no-one can be forced to learn if they choose not to, skilful developers find ways to build it into the system so that people get the learning 'habit'.

6. **Creating developmental opportunities is a prime responsibility of any manager. (Approved answer, yes.)**

Strictly speaking it isn't possible for a manager to take responsibility for anyone else's development, other than his/her own. This is why all development ultimately is self-development (see item 20). That said, the most a manager can and should do is provide ample opportunities for learning and development. Generating opportunities is what it's all about.

7. **Some people are incapable of further development. (Approved answer, no.)**

Of course, people may reach a ceiling in terms of potential and promotability, (even that is debatable; the ceiling may be in the eye of the beholder rather than real), but because development is an on-going process (see 2 above) it is unwise to succumb to defeatism. There is a very real risk of a self-fulfilling prophecy; if you expect someone to be incapable of development, they probably will be. People have an endless capacity to surprise us - if they are provided with appropriate opportunities.

8. **Most people respond best to praise and recognition. (Approved answer, yes.)**

Even the most self-assured, accomplished people appreciate recognition mainly because, in this punitive world, they don't get enough of it.

No doubt there are exceptions, but praising is a far more powerful motivator than criticizing. The trick is never to assume good behaviour and to put effort into catching people doing it right.

9.   **The best way to develop people is to let them have a go and learn from their mistakes. (Approved answer, no.)**

Undoubtedly mistakes, when they occur, and if handled properly, are splendid learning opportunities but they are only a fraction of the story. Successes and the myriad number of things that are neither obviously mistakes nor successes, are all grist to the learning and development mill. The best way to help people develop is to use a wide range of experiences that cover the whole spectrum.

10.   **It is up to managers alone to assess the strengths and development needs of their subordinates. (Approved answer, no.)**

Everyone is responsible for assessing their own strengths and development needs. The managers' perceptions are an important part of the picture which is why it is vital that managers give their subordinates feedback. It would be arrogant in the extreme for managers to act as both judge and jury.

11.   **Development is best done in the work place. (Approved answer, yes.)**

This links back to item 4 and the points already made about the advantages of work-based learning and development. What happens day in and day out on-the-job is a far more potent contributor to someone's development than attending the occasional off-the-job course or conference. Work-based learning is the key.

12.   **Developing people inevitably raises false hopes and expectations of promotion. (Approved answer, no.)**

Someone might get the wrong idea and imagine that he/she is being groomed for promotion but it certainly isn't inevitable. The whole purpose of development is to help someone improve their *current* performance. Doing so might or might not lead to subsequent promotion. The thrust of development is always to get the most out of 'here and now'. Future promotion is a different issue and depends on other factors such as the availability of an opening.

13. **It is just as important to learn from successes as it is to learn from mistakes. (Approved answer, yes.)**

This links back to item 9. By and large people get things right more often than they get things wrong and learning from the things that happen frequently is every bit as important as learning from relatively infrequent mistakes. Mistakes often have a greater impact than successes but that is only because we allow them to. Paying as much attention to learning from successes would help to redress the balance.

14. **No matter how expert someone is, there is always room for improvement. (Approved answer, yes.)**

Experts are people who have made more mistakes than anyone else - and learned from them. Complacency is one of the hazards of being an acknowledged expert. It is easy to be lulled into a sense of false security and to stop continuously striving to improve. Complacency is the biggest single enemy to the process of learning and continuous improvement.

15. **Most people respond best to criticism and/or the threat of unpleasant consequences if their performance is unsatisfactory. (Approved answer, no.)**

This links back to item 8. Criticism and sanctions are fine so long as they are outweighed by praise and recognition. All the evidence suggests that people develop best by building on strengths and emphasising the positive. Criticism, when it is appropriate, has a legitimate part to play but punitive regimes breed cautious people who are continually looking over their shoulders. Defensiveness militates against learning and development.

16. **Managers cannot *make* people develop - only make it more likely that they will. (Approved answer, yes.)**

It is not possible to force someone to develop, only to make the prospect of continuous learning and development so attractive that he/she *wants* to do it. As we shall see, building learning opportunities into the everyday working environment is part of what is involved in making it likely that people will want to develop. You can lead a horse to water but you can't force it to drink.

17. **The best way to develop people is to set them a challenge on a 'sink or swim' basis. (Approved answer, no.)**

'Sink or swim' implies leaving people entirely to their own devices with no assistance. This is too risky. A lot of people will sink for want of a little help. There is nothing wrong with setting people developmental challenges but they work best if you provide help, such as feedback and coaching, rather than leaving people to struggle unaided.

18. **The prime purpose of development is to help everyone continuously to improve their performance. (Approved answer, yes.)**

This links back to item 3. The *whole* purpose of development is to help *everyone* continuously to improve.

19. **Some jobs are so routine and prescribed that they offer no learning opportunities. (Approved answer, no.)**

Jobs vary from the complex and ambiguous to the routine and prescribed, but to believe that a job offers no learning opportunities is a shameful admission of defeat. The challenge is to see how to enrich routine jobs so that they have developmental potential for the job holders.

20. **Ultimately everyone has to take responsibility for their own development, ie all development is self-development. (Approved answer, yes.)**

There is no alternative to taking responsibility for your own development. No-one else can do it for you and you cannot do it for anyone else. This is why all development is self-development.

What's in it for you, the manager?

If you can't see real advantages in helping your people to develop the chances are you won't do it, or you will just pay lip service to the concept. It is easy to appreciate how the people who are being helped to develop will benefit, but what's in it for you? Let's be selfish and look at it purely from your point of view. In no order of importance here are three utterly selfish reasons to develop your people.

1.   To reduce your vulnerability.

     All managers are vulnerable simply because they are dependent on their subordinates for their results. A manager, by definition, has too big a job to accomplish alone; that is why he/she has subordinates to assist. So your results depend, to a greater or lesser extent, on the performance of your subordinates. Clearly the more you help them learn and develop, the better their performance is likely to be and the less vulnerable you will become.

2.   To get people to learn what you want them to learn.

     People learn whether you want them to or not. As we have already seen, it's foolhardy to let 'automatic' learning run its course with no controls, constraints or influences. It is too easy for people to learn unhelpful things like, for example, pretending that all is well when it is not, censoring bad news, covering up mistakes and many more behaviours like these that make life more difficult for you. So, since learning is unstoppable you might as well harness the process and turn it to your advantage.

3.   To develop yourself and make your life more interesting.

     The act of helping other people develop in itself increases your own learning opportunities. There is a quantum leap in the number and frequency of situations from which you can derive personal learning. Suppose, just to take one example, that you experimented with 'stretch delegation',

9

ie empowering someone to carry out a task on your behalf which is a little bit beyond his/her current capabilities. You stand to learn lessons about who can take what amount of 'stretch', when to let go and empower and when to check and intervene and so on and so on. Lessons galore which help you to increase your effectiveness as a manager.

What are the consequences of not helping your people to develop?

Even if you are doubtful that you would enjoy the advantages, at the very least you might want to avoid the perils of not helping your people to develop. Consider the following list:

You'll have

- less competent subordinates
- a continual struggle to make up for people's deficiencies
- the frustration of the same mistakes happening over and over again
- subordinates who pull the wool over your eyes and fob you off with excuses
- over-dependent rather than independent (or better still, inter-dependent) subordinates
- an exodus of your best people
- people who are cautious and cling to the status-quo and resist change
- a constant need to check, double check and intervene
- the horrible feeling that things are out of control and that you are running hard but going backwards.

Not a nice list. Surely, even if you are a cynic, it would be better to indulge in some damage limitation by developing your people?

How can you develop people *without really trying?*

The answer is right under your nose and always has been. Use everyday 'normal' events as developmental opportunities. Simply piggyback development on the shoulders of activities that in any case have to be done. This saves time and money and has the massive advantage of killing two birds with one stone; tasks are accomplished whilst development is guaranteed.

10

Of course you can supplement everyday opportunities with some 'extras' that are more lavish and contrived - but the first priority is to get developmental mileage out of 'ordinary' inexpensive things.

In a sense *everything* you do as a manager has developmental implications for your people. It just helps if you do things knowing this, rather than leaving development to chance or running the risk of sending out conflicting signals.

1   Acting as a sounding board

Strictly speaking a sounding board doesn't speak; it just amplifies noises that come from someone, or something, else. Acting as a sounding board is extraordinarily difficult for most managers - especially if they regard it as their role to be the fount of all wisdom, at all times, to know what's best. Letting people think out loud so that they resolve their own problems and reach their own answers is a valuable and grossly under-utilized process. The very act of having to turn previously shadowy ill-formed thoughts into words clarifies issues without the need for intervention from anyone else, however well intended. So, in a sense, sounding boards amplify learning.

Being a sounding board does not mean doing nothing (though just being there while someone talks is better than nothing). The most effective sounding boards go in for active, as opposed to passive, listening. In essence active listening means doing the following things

- giving the speaker your complete, undivided attention. You concentrate so hard that it's as though there is no-one else in the world

- listening, without any interruptions and without thinking about what you are going to say next

- making 'I'm listening' noises with accompanying nods of the head, eg umm, ah, I see, mmm

- occasionally paraphrasing what the speaker has said, eg 'So what you're saying is....' 'You seem to be concerned about....' 'As I understand it, your position is....' ' So from your point of view...'

- controlling all urges to make judgements, give advice, offer guidance or interrupt.

That's it! But, of course, like so many worthwhile interpersonal skills, these things are easier said than done.

Clearly, there is a time and place to act as a non-directive sounding board and a time and place to be directive, give guidance and generally be bossy. If only managers did more of the former and less of the latter, they would be far more helpful than they often are. If it is unclear what a person wants, ask them point blank 'Do you want me to give you advice or to act as a sounding board?' Even if he/she plumps for advice, you still need to employ your sounding board skills to understand the ins and outs of the situation before you are ready to offer appropriate advice. And before you get to that stage, the penny may have dropped and they may have reached their own conclusion. Notice how profusely they thank you, and all you did was enable them to do all the work.

2 Advertising lessons learned

People invariably claim to learn something new each day but are rarely required to describe exactly what they have learned. Pressing people to substantiate their claim almost seems like an incursion into private grief. It is easier to assume people are continuously learning from experience and let them get on with it. But to do so leaves whatever has been learned un-communicated with the risk that the learner him or herself isn't crystal clear and with the grave consequence that no-one else can benefit from it.

The solution is to establish communication channels where what your people have learned can be advertised for all to see. There are a number of ways to bring this about

- you could have a large notice board in a strategic place dedicated to learning. Anybody would be eligible to write a 'lesson learned' notice and post it on the board for all to see. The notice board would be cleared once a fortnight to encourage a constant flow of fresh notices

- you could have a monthly departmental circular where people submitted 'lesson learned' pieces

- if you have an E mail facility then lessons learned could be transmitted electronically rather than relying on old fashioned notice boards and circulars on paper

- you could instigate a fortnightly learner's corner (akin to speaker's corner) where at lunch time volunteers could get on a 'soap box' and give a five minute talk on some recent experience and what they had learned from it

- you could make it a routine requirement that all project teams, task forces and anyone given an investigative task have to include a full description of the lessons learned from tackling the project. This could be displayed alongside the recommendations themselves and given equal prominence

-   you could set up a learning scheme, similar to a suggestions scheme, where people put lessons learned notices in boxes which are processed by a democratically elected panel who 'judge' the quality of the entries against agreed criteria and award small prizes

-   you could set up learning circles, similar to quality circles, where people meet to swop experiences and identify lessons learned that would benefit them and the organization.

The purpose of all these ideas is to provide conduits where learning can be transmitted loud and clear so that your people become used to describing what they have learned and, above all, have the opportunity to learn from what other people have learned. Blowing the learning trumpet needs to become an accepted practice rather than something strange or unnatural.

3   Aiming high

As a manager, whether you recognize it or not, you are inevitably a trend setter. Your subordinates are constantly observing your behaviour and being influenced by it. They compare notes and decide whether you are being fair or unfair, consistent or inconsistent, open or secretive, straight or two-faced and so on. It is impossible to escape the scrutiny of your subordinates. You are a major factor in their lives.

It follows, therefore, that if you set high standards for yourself you become a role model for the people who work for and with you. Aiming high helps people develop because they have to strive to achieve high standards. The process of striving automatically generates more learning opportunities than would otherwise be the case.

Everyone has standards but it helps if you make yours explicit rather than tacit, and have a range of high standards across a broad band of categories rather than having one or two well known foibles that people regard as a bit of a joke. For example, you can have standards to do with

- professionalism
- equal opportunities
- the absence of sexual harassment/swearing
- personal integrity
- environmental issues
- tidiness
- punctuality
- the clarity of written memos, letters, reports
- grammatical correctness
- the frequency and thoroughness of performance appraisals
- the conduct of meetings
- confidentiality
- expense claims
- financial remuneration
- your availability
- saving energy/reducing waste
- meeting deadlines.

It doesn't of course follow that everyone will emulate *all* your high standards, but undoubtedly most people will aim higher than they would otherwise have done. Being a manager is rather like being a pace setter in a race; you set the pace to enable others to win.

The trick is to set high but attainable standards. If they are too challenging you will fail to match up to your own rhetoric and lose credibility as a consequence. Standards that are perceived as unattainable turn people off and prevent the striving that creates learning opportunities.

4   Analysing mistakes

Mistakes are inevitable and have the potential to be admirable learning opportunities. A mistake is likely to 'bounce' someone into learning mode in a bid to avoid repeating the same mistake in future. However, learning is by no means inevitable. In the wake of a mistake people can react by

- denying it happened
- concealing/covering up the mistake
- rationalizing/explaining the mistake away
- blaming factors outside their control
- attacking other people for their mistakes
- confessing/coming clean
- apologising
- learning.

Alas, the first five are far more prevalent than the last three.

The way to maximize learning and development from mistakes is to lean over backwards to be non-accusational. The easiest way to do this is to concentrate on the only two things that really matter

- agreeing what action to take to alleviate the effects of the mistake

- agreeing what action to take to prevent the mistake happening again.

This problem-solving, action-oriented approach is much too businesslike to indulge in unhelpful trivialities such as apportioning blame and finger pointing. Rebuking people when they make mistakes doesn't necessarily mean they will make fewer mistakes in future. More probably it will encourage them to conceal their mistakes in order to avoid being rebuked. As every school child quickly learns, you don't get told off for making mistakes; only for being found out.

So, if mistakes, when they occur, are handled properly, development is the desirable outcome. This doesn't mean that mistakes are to be welcomed, or that efforts to prevent mistakes can be relaxed; merely that when they happen we might as well gain from them.

It is possible, indeed desirable, to learn from other people's mistakes rather than restricting it to the ones that happen in your sphere of influence. Analysing accident reports or newspaper or magazine articles about other organizations, products or personalities can often be a useful exercise. Important and relevant lessons can be extracted from case-study material of this kind without the pain of having made the mistake yourself. A good place to start would be the paperback published by Butterworth Heinemann called 'My Biggest Mistake' where captains of industry admit to a substantial mistake and describe the lessons they have learned from it. Once people have got into the spirit of things, you can move the process closer to home by having your own equivalent (see 25, Confessing).

Whether it is your mistake, your subordinate's mistake or someone else's mistake, always remember 'inside every mistake are lessons waiting to get out'.

5   Answering questions

The answers you give to people's questions have the capacity to help or hinder their development. Questions are asked in order to solicit answers from which people can learn (except in the House of Commons where questions and answers are reduced to point-scoring ploys).

Answering questions in a way that aids learning and development has three different aspects.

1. Exposing yourself to questioning
2. The quality of your answers
3. The extent to which your answers are understood by the questioner

You have to take responsibility for all three aspects, not just the second one.

If you don't behave in ways that actively invite questions, then people may hold back and not ask the questions they would like to for fear of appearing foolish. Try having regular question and answer sessions where people can come prepared with questions. Even the act of *inviting* questions, as opposed to assuming people will be brave enough to ask them if they want to, sends out a signal that asking questions is OK.

There are a number of inter-related criteria to determine the quality of your answers

- how much *new information* the answer contains for the questioner

- the extent to which the answer is *relevant* to the questioner

- the extent to which the answer is *useful* to the questioner.

The higher your answers can score on all three counts, the better their quality from a developmental point of view.

The final aspect, that is all too easily overlooked, is to check that your answer has been understood. The onus is always on you, the communicator, to do this. People will often pretend they are clear when in fact they are not. The surest way to test understanding is to ask the questioner to summarize what they have just understood from your answer (see 93, Testing understanding). If people know you are prone to doing this, it is an additional incentive for them to listen hard to your answers.

6   Anticipating consequences

Left to their own devices, most people aren't in the habit of looking ahead and anticipating the consequences tomorrow of an action taken today. There are numerous examples of this. The 'M25 effect', for example, where the consequences of building the orbital motorway around London were not anticipated, ie that its very existence would create extra traffic. Or the effect of teaching children to swim in swimming pools. Apparently this increases their confidence with the consequence that more drown in rivers and the sea where conditions are quite different from those encountered in indoor pools. Or, to give one more example, the effect of improved health care and increased longevity on government expenditure; nearly half the social services budget goes on benefit expenditure to the elderly, and it's rising.

Helping people to think ahead and anticipate the consequences of their behaviour provides them with a learning opportunity which is often salutary. For a start it weans them off short-termism, quick fixes and the tendency to go for immediate gratification. Secondly, it forces them to think things through *before* taking action. Thirdly, it makes it easier to learn from a comparison of the consequences that were anticipated and the ones that actually occurred. Last, but not least, the whole exercise will often mean that an intended action is significantly modified, or even abandoned, once likely consequences have been identified.

So, a bit of crystal ball gazing never did anyone any harm and, especially for people who tend to be gung ho, developing the habit of looking ahead is very useful.

There are two simple ways to get people to anticipate consequences. One is to keep asking, 'if we do this, what do you think the consequences will be?' Asking the question acts as a trigger for forward thinking and, who knows, if you keep asking the question people might start to anticipate it.

Secondly, you can invite people to take part in 'what if-ing?' exercises. What if interest rates fall/increase? What if there is a power failure? What if there is a fire? What if such and such a person leaves? What if our competitors cut their prices? What if there is global warming?

Any circumstance, large or small, can be 'what if-ed' with the double advantage of having contingencies worked out just in case, and having forced people to practise looking ahead and anticipating consequences.

7   Appraising

Appraisals are invariably unpopular mainly because they are a device for forcing reluctant managers to sit down and discuss a subordinate's performance at least once a year. No-one likes to be coerced into doing something they'd rather not do and appraisals often fall into this category, especially where they are seen as part of a bureaucratic system. The answer, of course, is to adopt the practice of having frequent mini-appraisals with your subordinates so that the annual appraisal just becomes a formality.

Appraisals, done properly, are an honest attempt to review someone's current performance and help them identify how best to improve. The accent is on *current* performance not speculations about someone's potential. Learning and development is always about the 'here and now' as the best investment for the future.

There may be a number of reasons why you are reluctant to appraise your staff

- fear of upsetting the appraisee
- fear of sounding condescending
- feeling once removed and unsure of the 'facts'
- subordinates who are defensive or touchy
- subordinates who seem self-sufficient
- subordinates who never solicit feedback
- lack of skill.

Undoubtedly the easiest way to overcome any reluctance on your part is to arrange things so that your subordinates take the initiative and ask you for an appraisal. Proactive subordinates, determined to extract every bit of help from you, wouldn't hesitate to assert their right to feedback. Less assertive subordinates will need your active encouragement to take this bold step. An excellent way to bring this about is to solicit feedback from them on *your* performance (see 95, Upward appraisal/feedback) thus making it more likely that they will ask you to reciprocate.

If, after suitable encouragement, your subordinates fail to solicit appraisals then you must take the initiative, override your doubts, and offer feedback. The soundest way to do this is to give feedback against some agreed standards of performance; praise when the performance matches or exceeds the standards and criticism when it does not (see 70, Praising and 30, Criticizing). The agreed standards make the whole process less invidious and less dependent on personal whims and perceptions. Often an appraisal discussion will result in the clarification of an existing standard or the creation of a new one and in this way perceptions of what is expected of the subordinate will gradually coincide. Top priority, however, is that each appraisal discussion results in an action plan to improve some aspect of the subordinate's performance and, preferably, that you too come away from the encounter having committed yourself to further actions that will support the subordinate in his/her quest for continuous improvement.

If you are serious about helping your subordinates to learn and develop you will be a regular and frequent appraiser.

8   Asking for advice

Every time you ask someone for advice you are providing them with an opportunity to contribute and become more involved than would otherwise be the case. You don't necessarily have to take the advice (though sometimes you might find it sufficiently helpful and wish to do so); it is simply enough to have asked for it.

Asking for advice triggers learning in a number of ways. Firstly, it increases empathy by getting the other person to appreciate things from your point of view. Your adviser needs to put him/herself in your shoes and to see where you are 'coming from'. The ability to empathize is thus practise. Secondly, it increases analytical skills by providing your adviser with the opportunity to ask probing questions to increase their understanding of your situation. Exploring someone else's problem is always rich in learning, partly because of the skills involved in 'getting to the bottom' of things and partly because, in the process, the adviser might discover some salient facts they had not previously known or appreciated. Thirdly, asking for advice provides your adviser with an opportunity to practise his/her skills of persuasion. Whenever someone gives advice, they have the challenge of making it as attractive and acceptable as possible to the receiver of the advice.

So, the simple act of asking for advice is, from a development point of view, a nugget. In a way, the more ignorant and uninformed the person whose advice you seek, the greater the gain from a learning point of view. It is surprising how often someone with a fresh perspective comes up with the germ of a good idea. Even if they don't, it is still worth asking for their advice in order to give them the opportunity to practise the skills listed above.

Asking for advice can be done anywhere at any time. Some people will benefit by being given advance warning and time to collect their thoughts, other people will benefit from something more spontaneous.

There are two perils to guard against which risk diminishing the learning. The first is to ask for advice in a way that sounds as if you have already made up your mind and are merely testing the adviser to see if he/she reaches the same conclusion. If this is the case, then it is far better to come clean, explain your preferred solution and invite them to offer their comments.

The second peril is, having asked for advice, to pour scorn on whatever is forthcoming. It is often tempting to be dismissive (especially if you are better informed than the person whose advice you are seeking) but it risks destroying the whole process. People are unlikely to proffer advice if they find doing so is a bruising experience. You must make sure, therefore, that when you ask for advice you are doing so with the motive of generating a developmental opportunity and not with the hidden motive of showing how clever you are by rubbishing the advice you sought.

Asking advice from a subordinate gives a clear indication that you value that person's opinion and is likely to increase his/her commitment. If, at the same time, you provide a learning opportunity, you must be on to a winner.

9   Asking questions

Questions stimulate the mind and give people the opportunity to think things through.   Questions are powerful because they demand answers and most people find them irresistible.   Even when people don't know the answer, the compulsion not to leave questions unanswered is strong enough to provoke curiosity and investigations that wouldn't have happened if the question hadn't been posed.

Asking questions is an under-rated skill with the potential to kill two birds with one stone; to help the person being questioned to learn and to provide you, the questioner, with answers from which you can learn.   A classic win-win if ever there was one.

Questions come in all sorts of shapes and sizes.   There are questions to

- get ideas ('How could we solve that?')

- get a reaction to ideas ('What do you think of that?')

- check whether someone is in agreement ('Do you agree?')

- clarify something ('Do you mean...?')

- get information ('What is today's date?')

- get opinions ('What views do you hold on capital punishment?')

- find out somebody's needs ('What colour would you prefer?')

- identify a problem ('How often does he do that?').

Most questions fall into two broad categories; closed questions aimed at extracting one piece of information quickly without inviting further discussion, and open questions aimed at eliciting more expansive answers and encouraging further discussion.

Closed questions can be answered with a simple yes or no ('are you feeling fit?') whereas open questions cannot ('how are you feeling?').

Open questions are better for encouraging learning and development. They invite the other person to participate and 'think aloud'. The act of expressing opinions and ideas in response to open-ended questions, focuses what would otherwise be fuzzy, vague and ill informed thoughts.

The secret of success is to avoid rhetorical questions that don't require an answer at all, and to practise converting closed questions into open ones. This isn't as easy as it sounds. Managers ask interrogative, closed questions far more often than they ask expansive, open ones. Here are some examples of how to turn closed questions into open ones.

Closed questions	Open questions
Are you responsible for quality?	How do you ensure quality?
Did you double check the invoice?	What is the process for checking invoices?
Have we received the supplies yet?	When are the supplies due to arrive?
Did the meeting start on time?	What time did the meeting start?
Is that the time?	What is the time?
Should we inform personnel?	Who should we inform?

If you prefix a question with how, what, where, when or who, you will invariably ask an open-ended question. The other vital discipline is to confine yourself to one question at a time. Multi questions are inefficient (people rarely remember to answer all the questions) and often slide from an initial open question to a less useful closed one, for example 'How do you ensure quality? Is each person responsible for checking their own invoices? Or is it done by quality control?' An admirable open question sunk without trace by two consecutive closed ones.

If people can't immediately answer your questions that's no bad thing (it means you have asked a good one), but do get people to commit themselves to providing you with an answer by a reasonable deadline. Remember the deadline and chase them for an answer if it isn't forthcoming.

Finally, here are two splendid questions to aid people's development

-    what have you learned today?

-    what are you going to do better/differently tomorrow?

These two questions bear repetition. If people expected to be asked them, they'd soon learn to have some ready answers and that alone would help to put learning and development on the conscious agenda.

10 Audio tapes

Listening is an obvious way to learn (see 57, Listening) and that includes listening to tapes. Since so many people have cassettes for playing music in their cars, at home, when commuting, jogging and walking it would be a wasted opportunity not to use tapes as a learning aid.

There are audio tapes available commercially, just like videos (see 94, Training videos), on a wide range of topics and they are comparatively inexpensive. You can even pay an annual subscription to get tapes through the post monthly just like subscribing to a trade journal or magazine.

Much more exciting, however, is the prospect of making your own tapes that people can hear in their own time or as they travel. No great skill or complicated technology is required to produce a homespun audio tape that conveys useful information. Just think of the possibilities; you could

- produce a weekly tape briefing and updating your people on developments in your company or department

- expound your philosophy and approach on a whole variety of work- related topics

- get your boss or your boss's boss or the CEO, or whoever, to explain recent events and their vision for the future

- record an important conversation or meeting and send it out on tape, rather than depend on circulating written minutes of the proceedings or a second-hand account

- record a keynote speech by a senior manager or visiting dignitary or outside consultant and circulate it so that your people can eavesdrop rather than depending on a *précis* of what was said

- record a relevant programme from radio (or

television) on some current affairs item that has a
bearing on your business

- have a monthly magazine programme where people
  in your department contribute items of information
  they wish/would like to communicate to others

- get different groups within your department to
  contribute to a 'getting to know us' tape

- have an induction tape for new starters about the
  work of the department, its objectives, the key
  players, etc.

- get new starters to make a tape introducing
  themselves; who they are, their previous experience,
  their skills and areas of expertise, their hobbies and
  outside interests

- get people who retire to make a tape of
  reminiscences about how it was in the 'good old
  days', how things have changed and what they hope
  to achieve in their retirement

- get anyone who achieves something or has learned
  something from a recent experience to talk about it
  on tape so that others can benefit.

No shortage of ideas about how to use audio tapes to aid learning.
There is much to be learned from making tapes as well as from
listening to them. Basic communication skills, such as deciding
what to include, putting it across in a clear, succinct and
interesting way, are all involved and many people who tend to be
reticent find it easier to project themselves indirectly on tape
rather than in person.

Who knows, once you've conquered audio tapes there could be a
clamour to progress to making your own videos.

11 Being curious

Curiosity is supposed to have killed the cat, but only after it had used up nine lives. Being inquisitive and interested in people, things and events is an admirable characteristic, both because it increases your own learning and also because it is infectious. If you display curiosity, the people around you will be more curious then they would otherwise have been.

An open, enquiring mind is a pre-requisite for continuous learning and development. The alternative, a closed mind, is a recipe for stagnation and for the rate of change to exceed the rate of learning.

If you are not already the sort of person who displays curiosity, it is possible for you to learn to become so. How easy or difficult this will be depends on your starting point. If you *feel* curious, interested and inquisitive but don't *behave* it, then it is comparatively easy to adopt some behaviours that will demonstrate your curiosity. You could, for example, have a policy where you talk to people about what interests them, ask loads of questions and declare overtly how interested you are. These behaviours will obviously be quite easy to adopt if you are already half way there by feeling interested. It will undoubtedly be more difficult to display these behaviours if in fact you don't *feel* interested. However, all is not lost because it is quite possible to feign interest even if you don't initially feel it. Most people discover that if they pretend to be interested, then, lo and behold, they start to feel interested. The outward behaviour affects the inner feelings rather than the other way round.

You want to instil a sense of curiosity into your people because it provides the springboard for their learning and development. Curious, inquisitive people

- ask lots of questions
- think out loud
- play devil's advocate
- dig and delve to find out more
- formulate, and reformulate 'theories'
- have lots of ideas
- challenge conventional thinking
- are bubbly and enthusiastic.

An admirable list. The down-side, however, is that people who are curious will often flit, butterfly-like, from one interest to another and not sustain their enthusiasm and see something through to a conclusion. They are good starters but poor finishers. You can correct this tendency by maintaining *your* interest and continually checking to ensure that your people are completing whatever they've started.

Consistent curiosity is what is needed; the life blood of continuous improvement. All learning and development emanates from an insatiable curiosity.

12 Benchmarking

Benchmarking is the process of comparing your methods, procedures, products and services with those considered to be better than yours.   This can happen in a parochial way by comparing one person's *modus operandi* with that of a more experienced or successful performer. It can happen *within* an organization where one function or department benchmarks itself against another, and it can happen *between* organizations by, for example, making comparisons with a 'best in class' competitor.

Whatever form it takes, benchmarking is an excellent way to generate learning. There is no perception without contrast (ie you can't really know what it feels like to succeed unless you have experienced failure) and benchmarking is guaranteed to reveal plenty of contrasts.

Any activity, big or small, lends itself to benchmarking. You could, for example, compare record-keeping procedures, appraisal schemes, disciplinary procedures, the conduct of meetings, the performance of teams and project management. Nothing is immune, though clearly it is best to focus on aspects of performance which are judged to be critical for success. Basically once you've decided what to benchmark you go through a five step procedure.

1.   Measure your own performance in the area selected for scrutiny

2.   Measure the performance of the best in class inside or outside your organization

3.   Assess the gap in your performance

4.   Develop an action plan to close the gap

5.   Implement the plan and monitor the results

Benchmarking has to be a continuous activity because nothing stands still and best practice today becomes ordinary, unremarkable practice tomorrow. Benchmarking also lends itself to a bit of imagination. Instead of measuring yourself against the obvious comparisons, a similar function or self-evident competitor, there is much to learn by comparing your processes with those of people who work in quite different spheres. If, for example, you work in a manufacturing organization, you could benchmark against a service organization. If you work in the private sector, you could benchmark against a public sector organization. If you work in a profit-making enterprise, you could benchmark against a voluntary, non-profit-making organization. The greater the contrast, the more there is to learn.

Not only can you benchmark against anyone else's processes, you can also get anyone to tackle it and thereby provide them with a developmental opportunity. Benchmarking is a project in its own right (see 74, Project work).

13 Brainstorming

Brainstorming is a specific technique, with its own rules and procedures, designed to create a temporary haven where it is OK for people to come up with off-the-top-of-the-head ideas. The whole idea is to give people 'permission' to go at risk and blurt out ideas with no fear of ridicule or retribution.

Clearly the main purpose of brainstorming is to generate lots of different ideas in a short time but it also provides people with an opportunity to learn a number of useful things. When brainstorming people have the chance to discover

- how people perceive what is ostensibly the 'same' problem in quite different ways

- the usefulness of the prefix 'how to' as a way of guaranteeing a helpful open-ended question that solicits more ideas

- the importance of having rules that everyone is clear about and a chairperson who ensures they are adhered to

- the importance of listening to other people's ideas and cross-fertilizing

- how difficult it is to suspend judgement when listening to *other people's* ideas

- how difficult it is to suspend judgement with *your own* ideas, ie not to censor them

- how vital it is to support and develop other people's ideas instead of finding fault with them (you don't require much of a brain to come up with reasons *not* to do things)

- why idea generation and idea evaluation are best kept separate (the former requires right brain thinking and the latter left brain thinking)

- why it is important to see the ideas recorded in

writing and not just to listen to them

- how it is possible to generate 100 ideas in 15 or 20 minutes

- how, even when all ideas have apparently been thought of, it is possible to squeeze some more out by forcing a connection between two unrelated ideas

- how creativity can be artificially induced by formal procedures rather than depending on people being in the mood (ie the techniques make the mood, not the other way round)

- why it is crucial to write up verbatim what someone says rather than a summary of one-word bullet points

- how the presence of a sceptical boss who 'knows all the answers' inhibits the flow of ideas.

A vast array of learning points all drawn from one short activity. If brainstorming can also succeed in contributing to problem solving then it has to be a highly recommended practice on both counts. A classic example of getting double mileage out of one technique.

If you are unsure how to set up a brainstorming session, here is a simple description of the stages involved:

1. The chairperson states the problem

2. The group joins in restating the problem, listing statements in the form of 'How to...?'

3. The group selects a basic restatement and the chairperson writes down 'In how many ways can we...?'

4. The chairperson explains and displays the brainstorming rules

   Think wild
   Cross-fertilize

Suspend judgement
Go for quantity

5.   The group do a warm-up session on a neutral problem - 'Other uses for a ...?'

6.   The group brainstorm

     Aim for 100 ideas in 20 minutes
     Display ideas on flip-charts
     Number each idea
     Include 30-second silences to aid cross-fertilization

7.   The chairperson selects the wildest idea 'Let's see if we can make something of...?'

If you want to make brainstorming an even richer development opportunity than it already is, rotate the chair and give different people a go on different occasions.

14 Briefing

Briefing, orally or in writing, is the process of keeping people up to date with events. Whenever you brief, you are automatically running a mini-training session.

The information you include in a briefing falls broadly into two categories. There is information people *need to know* in order to do their jobs properly. This is essential, non-negotiable data without which people's performance would be impaired. The other information is best described as *nice to know*. The *nice to know* category covers a broad spectrum of possibilities from titbits of extra information which are by no means essential, to data that puts the *need to knows* into perspective by giving additional whys and wherefors.

From a development point of view it is impossible to over-communicate. As oxygen is to fire so information is to learning. You should always err on the side of providing too much information. Even if unwittingly you overload people, you give them the opportunity to sort out the wheat from the chaff and that in itself is a learning opportunity!

Briefing is a developmental opportunity not just because information is conveyed, but also because people have to

- listen or read
- understand
- interpret
- ask questions
- decide how to use the information provided.

These are the fundamental skills that make communication between human beings possible, and every opportunity to give people practice in these skills should be seized and exploited.

Of course briefing, like any communication, is a two-way process; you brief them and they brief you. Both the briefer and the briefed have an experience from which to learn. One lesson to learn very quickly is that the onus is always on the person doing the briefing to transmit the information in such a way that it is received, ie understood and interpreted, as intended. Blaming the receivers of the communication for misinterpretations and 'getting the wrong end of the stick' is tempting but quite unfair. The briefer is always accountable.

To gain maximum learning benefit from briefings, they should be both frequent and regular. The best way to ensure this is to establish a formal procedure that gathers a briefing group together at fixed intervals, or a system for issuing written briefs on paper or via electronic mail. A cascading system, where one level briefs the next and so on down a hierarchy, ensures that managers brief regularly rather than leaving it to the vagaries of individual discretion. Either way, briefing is a chance to learn from the acquisition of new information and from the communication process itself.

15 Budgeting

There is much to learn from the whole discipline of forecasting how much money will be needed to fund an activity over a period of time, and then monitoring actual expenditure against the forecast. In many organizations, the budgeting process and financial reporting systems enjoy such high visibility that reputations are made or lost depending on budgeting skills.

If you are a budget holder, responsible for a cost centre or a profit centre, then you can provide your people with invaluable developmental opportunities by involving them in the processes you have to go through. You could involve them in all or some of the following

-       strategic planning and the identification of goals and objectives for the next year

-       determining the resources required to achieve the objectives

-       assessing current resources and estimating what additional ones are needed

-       reviewing variations in the existing budget and deciding their significance for the new budget

-       deciding what cushions it would be expedient to build into the budget

-       making contingency plans in case of upturns or downturns in performance

-       planning how to make a persuasive case and 'sell' the budget.

You might hesitate to involve your subordinates in these important, high profile processes but you, as the budget holder, retain overall control and the chances are that your subordinates will add value to the process. Even if they don't, you can console yourself that you provided them with a valuable learning opportunity and that, as a consequence, they will be more useful in the next round of budgeting.

Another possibility is to create mini-budgets under the umbrella of the main one and delegate responsibility for those. Taken to its logical extremes, every job holder could be a budget holder responsible for planning and managing their own budget. Not only would this increase their commitment, it would also make them better qualified to join you in creating the main budget. The organization's budgeting and financial reporting system could be replicated on a smaller scale within your own department. What better way to equip your people with such essential skills?

16 Building learning into the system

Things that depend solely on enthusiasm and will-power are rarely as robust as things that are driven by a 'system'. This is not to decry the importance of enthusiasm; merely to be realistic and to concede that it is unlikely that every manager in an organization will share an equivalent passion for learning and development. Even if they did, it would be necessary to support it with an infrastructure to ensure some standardization and sustainability.

Many of the ideas in this book would benefit from being institutionalized so that they happen 'automatically', because the system demands it, rather than being left to the discretion of individual managers.   For example, the ideas in section 2, Advertising lessons learned, which included

- having a learning notice board

- using electronic mail to transmit 'lessons learned'

- insisting that project teams report what they have learned alongside their recommendations

- having a learning scheme akin to a suggestions scheme

- having learning circles akin to quality circles.

All these ideas, and many others such as Appraising (section 7), Reviewing learning (section 78), Upward appraisal/feedback (section 95) are more likely to be sustained if they are built into the system so that no-one has to remember to do them. Another example of this approach would be to instigate a system where expense claims would only be eligible for payment if they were accompanied by a description of a recent lesson learned. The expense claim form could actually incorporate a perforated learning form and the process would dictate that expenses would only be reimbursed if the learning section had been completed.

Ideas such as these may be condemned for being unduly rule-bound and bureaucratic. The idea is to find ways to get learning and development to become a 'way of life'. The trick, of course, is to strike a balance between what is and what is not discretionary. The best rules

- are enforceable

- succeed in getting people to behave in the required way

- become (eventually) accepted as beneficial

- are regularly challenged to check their continued appropriateness and usefulness (see 18, Challenging).

Creating a learning regime with a solid bedrock of rules that meet these criteria would not only compliment individual enthusiasms, they might even prove inspirational.

17 Celebrating success

People get things right far more often than they get things wrong. Undoubtedly mistakes provide splendid opportunities for learning (see 4, Analysing mistakes) but so do successes. It is understandable why mistakes tend to receive more attention than successes; but you can easily redress the balance by 'catching people doing it right' and reinforcing success.

'One success leads to another' goes the old adage, but not if successes go unrecognized and the norm becomes the avoidance of mistakes. It is surprisingly easy for standards to drop and for people to assume that success means being cautious and careful and keeping out of trouble.

Even when people are successful, they often do not know why. It just seems like a fortuitous piece of good fortune. People who attribute success to luck are not learning the lesson Thomas Jefferson clearly had when he said 'I'm a great believer in luck, and I find the harder I work, the more of it I have'. More often than not people do not know why something they have done led to a successful outcome. The trick is to learn from successes so that they can be repeated and specific lessons learned from one success can be generalized to different circumstances.

There is plenty of learning mileage in celebrating successes. For example, people discover that

-       emphasising the positive is a far more powerful motivator than emphasizing the negative

-       no news, ie if no-one says anything then it must have been all right, is not good news

-       you win some, you lose some, but either way it's OK to 'go for it'

-       success is rewarded with the best reward of all; recognition

-       things are successful for a combination of reasons rather than there being one single factor

-   once you know the reasons for a success you can plan future successes even though the circumstances will never be identical

-   it isn't healthy to be inappropriately modest and 'hide your light under a bushel'

-   celebrating someone else's success gives vicarious pleasure from which everyone benefits.

A fair list of potential lessons from the delightful practice of celebrating successes. Make it a habit to find a success to celebrate, say, once a week and adopt the bottom line practice of ensuring that the ratio of recognizing successes to recognizing mistakes is at least 2 : 1.

18 Challenging

Everything can and should be challenged on a continuous basis. A lack of challenging leads to ossification, complacency and a lack of development. Not a pretty picture.

The whole idea of challenging is to stimulate thinking and to cause dissatisfaction. It may sound foolhardy to incite you to stir up dissatisfaction but it is a necessary pre-condition for any change. It is the juxtaposition of dissatisfactions (with current reality) and visions (of how much better things could be) that creates a positive desire to close the gap. No dissatisfaction, no change or at best trifling, cosmetic changes.

Essentially, challenging is about playing devil's advocate, ie deliberately putting the opposing view by objecting to something to test out its soundness and/or to get it improved. You can challenge

- the assumptions that lie behind people's thinking

- the beliefs that lie behind people's actions

- the appropriateness of people's behaviour in a given set of circumstances

- the methods, processes, procedures and rules that govern the way things are done.

Some of the most fruitful challenges are ones that go 'back to basics' and query undeclared assumptions or beliefs. For example, the assumption that people are basically passive, dependent and need external incentives to goad them into action, as opposed to the assumption that people are basically creative, active and want to do well. Or the belief that life should be fair and everyone should be treated equally. Or the belief that things should always be orderly, predictable and harmonious. There is no end to the possibilities. Even apparently straightforward attempts to describe a problem are worth challenging to check that it is the best one to solve. A famous example is where complaints about the length of waiting times for elevators in a plush apartment block led to the assumption that the solution lay in the installation of additional elevators; an expensive exercise. The assumption that there was 'no alternative' (how often have you heard that?) was challenged and the problem became 'how to reduce complaints about the length of waiting times for elevators?' The inexpensive solution was to install large mirrors in all the elevator lobbies. This gave residents something useful to look at while they waited and, psychologically, it seemed less irksome. Complaints plummeted.

Whenever you challenge your subordinates' assumptions, beliefs, behaviour or methods you are providing them with an opportunity to survive the objections and/or to further develop their ideas.

You can also reverse the process by inviting your subordinates to challenge you so that they learn the skills of playing devil's advocate (why should you have all the fun?) and you learn what it's like to be on the receiving end. All rules, regulations and procedures should be challenged at least annually to whip up dissatisfaction and a desire for change.

19 Championing change

Change and learning and development are inextricably interwoven; you can't have one without the other. People will often curse and swear about changes but there is no doubt they are superb generators of learning.

The most powerful changes are transformational where step by step modifications to the present situation are inappropriate. Transformational changes are big, complex and perplexing with ramifications that are difficult to predict. By contrast, incremental, step by step modifications to the present are relatively easy to predict and manage. Sometimes, however, a change that starts incrementally gains unexpected momentum and suddenly flips over and becomes transformational. A famous example is the Spinning Jenny invented by Hargreaves in 1764. This simple invention for spinning cotton eventually resulted in the Industrial Revolution (revolutions are always transformational). A current example might be the so-called Greenhouse Effect where global warming is so gradual that some people doubt it is happening at all. If and when deserts expand, ice caps melt and sea levels rise, the incremental changes will have become transformational.

Broadly there are two ways you can use change as a trigger for learning. Either you can be the initiator and champion change yourself and/or you can encourage your people to champion their own changes. From a learning point of view the latter is a more potent experience, though there is much to learn from having change imposed and the goal posts moved for you. Champions of change learn that

- the vision of how much better things could be has to be vivid and graphic to conjure up a clear, inspirational picture in people's minds

- resistance is inevitable and has to be managed

- there are different reasons for resistance and each needs a different strategy.

Reason for resistance	Strategy to overcome resistance
Parochial self-interest 'I will lose out'	Negotiate a win-win outcome
Misunderstanding 'I don't understand the reasons for this'	Inform and educate
Different perceptions 'We are doing it already' 'We've tried it before and it doesn't work'	Involve the resistors in participative sessions where differences in perceptions are explored
Low tolerance for change 'I dread anything that is unfamiliar/will spoil my routine'	Go ahead and impose the change but give resistors lots of support to help them discover the change isn't as bad as they feared

Other lessons about change will also be learned, such as 'there is nothing permanent, except change' and 'even transformational changes need incremental steps'.

Despite the rumour to the contrary, it is impossible to indulge in change for change's sake; at the very least you should indulge in it for learning's sake.

20 Clarifying values

Values are beliefs, often deeply held, about what is important. Everyone has developed a value system that encapsulates what they stand for and that they use to judge the world about them. Different values are the key to understanding why some people are passionate about environmental issues while others feel strongly about religion, politics, education, the family and so on. People bring their values to work and use them, rather like litmus paper, to test their experiences and decide what is satisfactory and what is unsatisfactory.

Whilst everyone has a value system, many people are unclear what they stand for and operate on an 'I'll know it when I see it' basis. Clarifying values makes it more likely that people will be principled and consistent and less enigmatic. Working with people who keep you guessing and who are difficult to fathom takes its toll. It is much easier to work with people when you know 'where they are coming from' and can count on a bedrock of consistency.

You can help your people clarify the values they have that affect their performance at work and, at the same time, give them a learning experience. Try the following as a way to start clarifying values.

1. Give your people a series of headings and ask them, independently without conferring, to select, say, three which are really important to them. Here are examples of useful headings for this purpose

    Ageism/racism/sexism
    Balance between work/home
    Equality/equal opportunities
    Fairness
    Management style
    Other people's standards/behaviour
    Openness/communications
    Participation/involvement
    Quality standards
    Recognition
    Rules
    The working environment

2.   For each of the three headings selected, ask each person, still without conferring at this stage, to write down a description of what they stand for, starting each with the prefix 'it is really important to me that...' (ie 'meetings start and finish on time', 'I am consulted on decisions that will affect me', ' people are honest and straightforward with me').

3.   Now, either in pairs or in small groups, encourage people to describe their values to each other. Values become clearer through a process of listening, explaining and justifying. The aim of the discussion is purely to clarify and not to persuade anyone to alter their values.

This process is greatly aided if you join in or, at the very least, if you have taken the trouble to write down some of your values so that your people know 'where you are coming from'.

There are many lessons to be gained from the process of clarifying values, amongst them being

-    a realization of the extent to which deep seated, unspoken values affect people's reactions, performance and behaviour

-    how values can be surfaced, shared and aired

-    how values, once made explicit, are capable of adaption and modification

-    how knowledge of someone else's values, even if they differ from your own, helps you to understand their actions (even if you don't approve of them)

-    how much easier it is to 'walk the talk' and be consistent if you know what 'the talk' is.

Everyone has values that markedly affect the way they react to the world about them. The process of clarifying these important but unseen influences is often tortuous but likely to generate many insights. Values definitely fall into the category of things that are 'better out than in'.

21 Coaching

Coaching is any discussion between you and a subordinate where the aim is to help him/her maintain and/or improve his/her performance. Coaching takes place on the job and assumes that people can learn from everything they do. Coaching is not issuing instructions, telling someone what to do or prescribing how to do it. It is about helping, guiding, encouraging, allowing space to perform and to do things differently.

The job of coaching is that it makes a direct contribution to getting the job done and, at the same time, with no extra effort, to the person's learning and development. The fascinating question is why, since coaching is self-evidently 'a good thing', it doesn't happen more? There are many possible reasons why you might not coach as often as you could. Here are some

- little or no commitment to developing your subordinates
- a dominant, directive style
- a perceived lack of time
- a lack of incentives to coach, ie you may work in an organization where there are no brownie points for coaching
- a lack of understanding of coaching and the skills involved
- capable subordinates seen as a threat
- an unwillingness to pass on or share information (eg a perception that knowledge is power)
- a fear of upsetting a subordinate
- previous failures 'I've tried it before and it doesn't work'
- an inability to recognize opportunities for coaching.

The last one, at least, is easy to put right. Numerous opportunities to coach arise in the normal course of events. For example when

- delegating
- discussing how to tackle a task or solve a problem
- implementing improvements to products, processes or services
- changing job responsibilities

- introducing changes to methods or procedures
- launching an individual or group project
- organizing deputising while you are away
- briefing and debriefing before and after attendance on a course.

You are probably already coaching without realizing that is what you are doing (like the man who discovered he'd been speaking prose all his life). All you have to do now is do it more consciously and more often.

As for the skills involved, they are all covered in different sections in this book. Listening,(section 57), Asking questions,(section 9), Testing understanding,(section 93), and Giving feedback, (section 43,) are the four key skills.

Those, plus a bit of empathy, ie saying things that show you understand what it's like to be in the other person's shoes, will stand you in good stead as a coach. They also double up as the skills you need when appraising (Section 7). An appraisal is just a bigger and more formal coaching session. If you have been a frequent coach, then the annual appraisal is a mere formality; a summary of the trends that have emerged from coaching sessions.

All this assumes that you are the coach helping someone else to learn. How about reversing the roles and getting your subordinates to coach you? (See 95, Upward appraisal/feedback).

22 Collaborating in decisions

Decision-making is a large part of any manager's job. You make a decision whenever you have to choose between two or more options and make up your mind what to do. Decisions might be trivial or important, repetitive or novel, expected or unexpected, easy or tortuous.

You can make decisions unilaterally or after a period of consultation or in collaboration with other people. Unilateral 'I' decisions may be convenient for you but they deprive other people of any involvement and therefore of a learning opportunity. Consultative decisions involve other people to the extent that you pick their brains before reaching your decision. This limited involvement is better than nothing but it still excludes people from the actual decision-making.

Collaborative 'we' decisions are undoubtedly preferable from a learning and development point of view because they involve people as equal partners in the decision-making process. This does not mean that all decisions should be collaborative. There is clearly a time and place for both autocratic and consultative decision-making, but if you want to develop people you would err on the side of collaborative decisions.

There are rich pickings to be gained from getting your people to collaborate in decisions. Here are some to whet your appetite and wean you off unilateral decisions taken behind closed doors:

People collaborating in decision-making are likely to learn

- the importance of spending time formulating the decision to be made or problem to be solved and the dangers of rushing headlong into a decision only to find you've solved the wrong problem

- how tempting it is to assume that there is a single right answer to all problems instead of lots of equally viable solutions

- how to tolerate the uncertainty of not knowing what the answer is while options are identified and ideas generated

- the importance of having agreed criteria against which to weigh and evaluate different options

- the importance of anticipating the consequences of a chosen course of action before implementing it

- that decision-making requires thought and is damned hard work

- that genuine consensus is rare and the perils of assuming that acquiescence is agreement

- that involvement increases ownership and commitment.

When you look at this list of potential lessons it is surprising that more managers don't indulge in collaborative decision-making. To do so is not a cop-out or an abdication of your managerial responsibilities because you are one of the collaborators. Who knows, you might even discover that the quality of the decisions is enhanced. Even if they are not, you still stand to gain from extra commitment and the continuous development of your subordinates.

23 Compiling scrapbooks

Scrapbooks can be fascinating collections of photographs, drawings, pieces of verse, thought-provoking sayings, clippings from newspapers or magazines. The idea of grown-ups compiling scrapbooks at work, as opposed to kids doing so in primary schools, may strike you as a little bizarre. And that's exactly its attraction; an unusual thing to be doing, which adds interest for all involved, and isn't distractingly time consuming.

It is vital to have a theme for your scrapbook project. There are any number of possibilities, for example

- items about your organization's products or services

- competitive information

- relevant financial and political news items

- items about markets and/or different overseas countries which could be future markets

- items about self-management techniques such as stress management, time management and so on

- items about the people in your department, their outside interests and hobbies

- future social trends which will have an effect on your business

- interesting quotes from management gurus

- cartoons which have a message for people in your organization

- collections of blunders, mistakes and *faux-pas* in the world of business and commerce

- statistics about this, that and the other that fall into a 'not many people know this' category.

You could either have a number of concurrent scrapbooks on the go with different themes or have a theme for a fixed period, say a quarter, before moving on to another one.

There are two main ways in which scrapbook projects aid learning and development. Firstly, the chosen theme gets people to notice things that would normally receive only cursory attention or be missed completely. The existence of the scrapbook provides a focus and helps contributors to tune their antennae. Secondly, reading through the scrapbook provides people with a valuable information source; your very own abstracts service.

There is also the added benefit of the scrapbook project being something to which everyone can contribute regardless of seniority or background. In fact, the greater the diversity of the contributors, the more interesting the scrapbook is likely to be. It's cheap too. An empty scrapbook is not likely to put much strain on your budget and, after the initial outlay, the contents are free.

24 Conducting surveys

Surveys are designed to gather information about something so that it can be carefully examined and, hopefully, improved. The whole process of deciding what to survey, how to survey, who to survey and when to survey is riddled with learning opportunities. Having conducted a survey, learning continues with the analysis and interpretation of the findings and, last but not least, decisions about what to do differently in the light of the results.

You can conduct surveys to find out

- what your customers, internal as well as external, think of the goods and services you provide

- the attitudes people in your organization have about a whole host of things such as pay and conditions, management style, business ethics and the food in the canteen

- the perceptions the general public have of your organization, your competitors or the business you are in

- people's needs, life styles, habits, interests and pastimes

- people's opinions about, well, anything you'd like to investigate - video nasties, abortion, divorce, chefs, the National Health Service, law and order, adult literacy, drugs.

The information can be gathered by questionnaires, telephone calls, and face-to-face interviews. The population to be surveyed can be randomly or systematically selected. The questions to be asked can be open-ended or force-choice. You don't necessarily have to do original research, although that is undoubtedly the most exciting; you could conduct a survey of other people's surveys into a subject area that interests you.

The whole process of gathering data and working out what it means generates some attractive learning opportunities such as

- planning the objectives of the survey, what data to collect and how

- deciding what questions to ask so that the data are not distorted and contaminated

- interviewing people in a standardized way (so that it's the same for all interviewees) to elicit comparable opinions

- using statistics to crunch the numbers and discover trends, correlations etc.

- interpreting the data and drawing conclusions from them

- producing recommendations about improved practices in the light of the survey findings

- presenting the results of the survey in a written report and/or in a presentation

- answering questions about the soundness of the survey design and the wisdom of the recommendations.

Conducting a survey and taking it through all its stages is, in effect, a mini project (see 74, Project work) and, like all projects, it has to be managed from its inception through to a conclusion.

All this activity, besides being interesting and worthwhile in its own right, provides a person, or more probably a small team, with a splendid learning opportunity. Getting outside agencies to conduct customer surveys passes up the chance to get your people close to their customers and to learn at the same time.

25 Confessing

In most organizational cultures confessing is rare and blaming is rife. This is because people have learned from numerous experiences that 'attack is the best form of defence' and that blaming other people, or 'circumstances beyond your control', invariably succeeds. A classic example of people learning to steer clear of trouble but in doing so, impeding progress and delaying the early identification of problems.

Helping people unlearn such an ingrained behaviour clearly presents quite a challenge. The key is to reverse the normal state of affairs and find ways to 'reward' confessing so that it becomes more attractive than blaming. One way to do this is to establish the equivalent of an amnesty for anyone who confesses early to a mistake, error or other misdemeanour. Clearly there would have to be some 'crimes' beyond the terms of the amnesty, such as stealing, but it only requires a little thought to decide what should and what should not be included.

Once people know they will not be punished for making early admissions to mistakes, you must launch the process by confessing yourself! Perhaps you have been too brusque with someone, or been unavailable, or been inconsistent or done something yourself that you should have delegated? Things, such as these, to do with your subordinates, lend themselves admirably to confessionals. Each confession should follow a fixed formula:

1. A brief description of the misdemeanour.
2. An apology.
3 A declaration of what you have done, or are going to do, to correct the situation now and in the future.

Whenever someone else makes a confession, you must make it a rule to ban any blaming or recriminations, and concentrate positively on the declaration to correct the situation by supporting or developing it into something even better.

Learning that it is OK to confess has considerable benefits both for the organization and for the individual. Admitting to inadequacies and failings is one of the hallmarks of a mature person. Developing the habit yourself is impressive. Helping your subordinates to become confessors is a massive contribution to organizational effectiveness, an essential ingredient in the process of continuous improvement and a development challenge second to none.

26 Consulting

Consulting isn't the same as collaborating. When you invite someone to collaborate it is a wholehearted invitation for them to join you as equal partners in the decision-making process (see 22, Collaborating in decisions). Consulting someone, however, invites less involvement on their part. In effect, you seek their opinions, advice and guidance but reserve the right to ignore the lot and make up your own mind.

People often mistake consultation for collaboration and finish up disappointed when the decision is taken without them and/or when the decision fails to take account of the advice proffered. But that's par for the course with consultation. You can reduce the likelihood of disappointment by making it clear at the outset that you are consulting not collaborating and spell out the difference between the two, ie that the former is an 'I' decision and the latter a 'we' decision.

Whatever the outcome, the process of consulting people generates many learning opportunities. They learn that

- you value their opinions and recognize that they have ideas to contribute

- the problems you grapple with as a manager are rarely straightforward and clear-cut

- it is OK to ask for help; even managers do it

- people have different perceptions of the problem and different points of view about the best way forward

- skills of persuasion are just as important as the quality of the ideas being put forward

- it is always worth having a go and trying to persuade someone to your way of thinking

- consultation isn't collaboration

- consultation is the basic building block in a democracy.

You can consult people singly or *en masse* as a group or in a meeting. The lessons learned from consultation tend to be enhanced if it is a group effort so long as there are ample opportunities for each person to have their say. If one or two strong minded vociferous people are allowed to hog the discussion, ideas from quieter people fail to materialize which diminishes the consultative process and the lessons learned from participating in it.

In summary, the more you consult your people, the better they will become at responding and the sooner you will be able to move them on to full blown collaboration.

27 Covering for holidays

Vacations, and other planned or unplanned absences, automatically provide opportunities for the people left behind. Take your job for example. Instead of giving it lock, stock and barrel to your obvious second-in-command, you could allocate different parts to a number of people in order to boost their development. Responsibility for your in-tray and routine correspondence could go to one person. Responsibility for signing off expenses and other bits of financial management to another person. Acting as your representative at various meeting could go to two or three people depending on the number of meetings and the extent to which the topics are mutually exclusive.

The development potential of your absences will become obvious once you start thinking of how to break up your job so that different parts can be temporarily allocated to different people. But of course it doesn't just have to be your job. Any absences by any of your staff provide similar opportunities for temporary job rotation and job enrichment. If you are going to be present while other people are absent you could afford to gamble and give people who appear quite unsuited to particular tasks, a go at them. No doubt they would require closer supervision but even this would create extra opportunities for coaching (see 21, Coaching).

Temporary absences are marvellous learning opportunities precisely because they are temporary. No-one is under any illusion of permanence. False hopes and expectations are unlikely when it is known from the outset that the real job holder will return after a week or two, or whatever. This is why you can afford to be bold and experiment by caterpulting people who would not normally get the chance, into more senior or more onerous positions. At the very least you'll discover whether they have what it takes to rise to the challenge and at best you'll give a quantum leap to their learning and development. And you might even find they do a reasonable job at covering for the absentee!

28 Creating your own workshop

Most workshops, conferences, seminars or courses are carefully contrived, structured and orchestrated. But it doesn't have to be like this. How often have you attended one of these events only to discover that you learned more during the coffee breaks than the formal sessions? This is not surprising. If you put like-minded people together with similar interests, learning from each other is the inevitable consequence. So here is how to design your own workshop without the need for pre-prepared topics or agendas.

1. Set aside some time, half a day minimum, one day maximum. Invite people to come with a current issue they would like to work on. The only criteria you need to provide are that the issues people bring should be

    -   work related

    -   generic rather than parochial or personal

    -   likely to be of interest to a number (not all) of the other participants

    -   genuinely still at a consultative stage, ie not a rubber stamping job.

2. Start the workshop by giving each participant a couple of minutes to 'advertise' their issue. Each issue should be written on a piece of flip chart paper and displayed on the wall.

3. Invite people to sign-up for an issue or two of their choice by writing their names on the appropriate pieces of chart paper.

4. Allocate a time (forty-five to sixty minutes) and a place for each viable topic.

5. Let people get on with it. As soon as someone finds they are not contributing or learning they are 'allowed' to move to another interest group (this is known as 'The Law of Two Feet', an expression coined by Harrison Owen, the inventor of Open Space Technology).

6. Finish your workshop with a swift wash-up session where a spokesperson from each interest group reports

    -       what was discussed
    -       what was decided.

That's it; your own homespun workshop guaranteed to be highly rated for relevance since the participants had total control over both issues and agenda. There is no need for speakers and all the other paraphernalia usually associated with organizing workshops, conferences or seminars. D-I-Y at its best.

29 Creativity

People often have jobs where opportunities to be creative are limited or non-existent. Some jobs have been routinized to such an extent that they only require people slavishly to follow laid down procedures. Other jobs leave people under-utilized for long periods of time. This can happen when people are in reactive as opposed to proactive jobs that require them to wait for something to happen. Secretaries, receptionists, security personnel, hotel and hospital porters immediately spring to mind.

It is easy for people who are not normally required to be creative at work to lose the sparkle and enthusiasm that creating something brings. Alternatively, they will find unhelpful outlets for their creative talents by, for example, finding and exploiting loopholes in rules and regulations or writing witty graffiti in the toilets.

Creative people are motivated people and if you have subordinates in jobs that don't, in the normal course of events, require creativity then you need to be creative yourself and think of ways to add in some opportunities to be creative. There are numerous ways this can be done. Here are some ideas to get you started

- challenge people to come up with unusual ideas for using the company's annual report

- get people to produce a brochure about your department and the staff who work in it

- each week cut out a photograph from a newspaper or magazine and have a competition to see who can produce the funniest caption

- have a competition to see who can produce an appropriate heraldic shield and motto for your department

- get people to produce ten minute presentations, complete with visual aids and other props, about their work

- have a competition to see who can produce the funniest cartoon about some recent aspect of organizational life

- get people to write rhyming couplets about recent events

- have an annual panto written and produced by people in your department

- have a competition to see who can compose the most uplifting company or departmental song

- appoint groups to be in charge of masterminding how to put across essential information in an attractive, effective way

- put people in charge of keeping notice boards up to date and interesting

- invite people to illustrate a report you've written.

When you run out of ideas you could further tap people's creativity by having a brainstorming session on additional ways to be creative at work (see 13, Brainstorming).

There are some important lessons to learn from creative activities. Firstly, the exciting discovery that people have so many skills and talents that were not previously apparent. Often individuals will claim they can't do something only to surprise themselves when they discover they can. Secondly, that creating together breeds mutual respect as people learn to value one another more. Thirdly, that work can be fun and that people are more productive and fulfilled when they enjoy what they do.

30 Criticizing

Whenever you criticize an action someone has taken you have given them a learning opportunity. Criticism is a legitimate form of feedback that needs to be balanced with the other side of the same coin; praise (see 70, Praising). It is the contrast between praise and criticism that makes both so effective. If you always praise and never criticize, people get used to it and come to expect it and the praise loses its potency. The same applies the other way round. If you over-indulge in criticism, to the detriment of praise, you get a reputation for your bark being worse than your bite and the impact is lessened.

One school of thought argues for a sandwich system where you start and finish with some praise and in between, as the 'filling', you have some criticism. In practice the problem with this is that it is too transparent. Everyone knows that the real purpose is to criticize and they downgrade the praise on the principle that 'everything before "but" is balderdash'. This is a wicked waste of praise; a rare enough commodity without tarnishing it with criticism. A better plan is, therefore, not to mix the two and to criticize and praise when each are deserved.

An obvious peril with criticism is that people will take umbrage and become defensive. This is particularly so if the criticism is perceived to be unjust and/or to be mistaken. The problem with defensiveness is that it saps the energy needed to convert the criticism into lessons learned. Of course there is supposed to be such a thing as *constructive* criticism. Whilst it is certainly true that criticism given skilfully is more likely to be regarded as helpful, it is always the perception of the person that determines whether it is constructive or destructive. You can help to tip the balance towards constructive criticism by adopting the following guidelines

-      always criticize the action not the person. This is more dispassionate and less accusational. Never criticize the person; merely something he/she has done that doesn't meet with your approval

-      always give specifics and avoid sweeping generalisations. It is detailed examples that contain the seeds of learning

-    always give suggestions on what the person can do to improve. Your ideas on possible ways forward are what makes the criticism constructive

-    always invite the other person to join you in thinking of ideas to improve the action, and avoid monologues where you do all the talking

-    always criticize assertively in an honest straightforward way. Avoid half truths and innuendos

-    always criticize in private and never in front of others. Public criticisms are counter-productive. They run the risk of humiliating the person and the bystanders tend to take sides.

Stick to these guidelines to make your criticisms a helpful learning experience for all concerned.

31 Customer focus groups

Being customer focused and listening to customers, internal or external, is much in vogue at present. It often proves a salutary experience when you discover that what the customers want does not necessarily match with what you thought they wanted. Gathering small, but representative, groups of customers together and getting them to talk is one of the best ways to find out what they really think.

Get your staff to invite some of their customers to a focus group at least twice a year. Put them in charge of the whole thing; fixing the venue, sending out invitations, structuring the session and processing and promulgating the data. Resist the temptation to sub-contract such a valuable experience to an outside consultancy or to marketing specialists. Your staff can learn so much from masterminding the session and, of course, from actively listening to feedback from their own customers. Here are some examples of what they stand to learn

- how to host a special customer event and demonstrate customer care throughout

- how to ask open-ended questions that get customers talking freely

- how to listen hard to what customers are saying, identify implications and innuendoes and ask supplementary questions to make them explicit

- how to resist the temptation to offer excuses and explanations and be defensive

- how to accept adverse, even unfair, feedback gracefully

- how to make copious notes on what customers say, verbatim, without interpretation, censorship or losing the details in summaries and afterwards,

-        how to analyse and categorize the notes and use the
         data as thought-starters to improve customer
         service.

There is no substitute to meeting face to face with customers and
finding out first-hand what they think of your products and
services. If you ensure that all your staff experience the process
at least twice a year you will have simultaneously struck a blow
for improved customer service and provided your subordinates
with a mini-project from which they can learn.

32 Cutting costs

Cost-cutting exercises are more likely to be considered a necessary evil than a learning opportunity. But *anything* that has to be done, nice or nasty, has learning potential.

From a development stand point involving people in decisions about what costs to cut is more fruitful than decisions taken unilaterally. The best way to do this is to give people a target, probably as a percentage reduction of current costs, and set them the challenge of deciding how best to achieve the target. It may be necessary to provide some ground rules or criteria, such as avoid cuts in expenditure that are likely to have an adverse effect on revenue, cash flow or profits. It is amazing how radical people can be with ideas on how to economize once they are convinced of the necessity and understand the constraints.

If parochial self-interest prevents subordinates from suggesting ways to achieve the cost-cutting target, then you can always intervene with something more ruthless. It is more likely that the need for this will be accepted if your subordinates have had the opportunity to generate ideas first. It is always easier to tighten the ratchet and to move from collaboration to consultation to direction than the other way round.

Lessons to be learned from cost-cutting exercises are many and various. Likely contenders include

- the importance of having unequivocal targets and constraints

- the ingenuity of colleagues in suggesting ways to cut costs

- a reappraisal of which activities are central and which peripheral

- a deeper understanding of the adverse consequences, on the bottom line and/or on morale and productivity, of cutting some costs

- trade offs between cutting some costs in order to increase expenditure in key areas of activity

- the worthwhileness of going back to basics and regarding everything as a legitimate area for exploration; that there are no 'no go' areas

- that everything is negotiable, nothing is sacrosanct.

Even if cost cutting is carried out unilaterally without involvement, there are lessons to be learned from the experience such as the differences in perception and priorities of people 'up there', the inappropriateness of cost-cutting decisions taken across the board regardless of local circumstances, the resistance unilateral decisions tend to evoke, how some decisions, even if unpopular, have to be autocratic.

Cost cutting is undoubtedly a salutary experience but, in common with so many salutary experiences, there is much to learn.

33 Debating

There have to be good reasons why schools, universities and other educational institutions have debating societies. It is because debating is a tried and tested formula from which there is much to learn. Marshalling arguments, both prepared and 'on the hoof', putting a case for or against, having your opinions challenged and casting a vote one way or the other are all fundamental democratic skills that have stood the test of time.

You can either set up formal debates on a range of contentious topics or use the debating process less formally within discussions and meetings. Suitable topics are anything where opinions are likely to be divided more or less equally. Examples are

- retirement ages should be lowered to alleviate unemployment

- top managers should have the same percentage salary increases as everyone else

- all companies should have workers on their boards of directors

- privatization is *the* way to improve an organization's performance

- open plan offices are more efficient than private offices

- everyone should eat in the same canteen regardless of seniority

- industry and commerce are over legislated

- company cars should only be provided to people whose job requires one

- mission statements are just empty rhetoric

- rules and bureaucracy are what keeps an organization together

-       all organizations have a built-in propensity to fail.

Probably the best way to enhance learning from debates is to give advance warning of the topic or 'motion' and to designate leading speakers for and against who have pre-prepared their opening remarks.   The leading speakers do not necessarily have to represent the argument with which they agree; there is more to learn from having to advance the opposite case with apparent conviction.

Encouraging debates on contentious work topics gets all the issues out into the open, thoroughly aired, and is an admirable way of 'taking the temperature' and seeing which way people's attitudes are inclined.   Whether you do this as a means of collaborative decision-making (see 22, Collaborating in decisions) or purely as an academic exercise, learning and development for all participants is guaranteed.

34 Debriefing

After someone has done something there is an understandable tendency to rush on to the next task. This is especially so when things have gone well or seem unremarkable. Rushing on may sound commendable *except* that it leaves the previous experience un-trawled for lessons learned. It is difficult for busy people, left to their own devices, to make time to hold post mortems. You need to condone the process and ensure it happens.

You, the manager, are in an ideal position to provide the necessary help. Firstly, you can insist on being debriefed and therefore force the person to pause and run over what happened. Secondly, you can ask pertinent questions and therefore force the person to think harder about their experience and what they have learned from it. What's more, adopting this simple routine also means that you are kept in touch rather than losing track of what is happening.

On all counts the most useful debriefs are ones where people tell it the way it really was, rather than trying to pull the wool over your eyes. The extent to which they feel they can be honest depends more on you and your behaviour than on them. Even the most reticent person can open up if you handle them appropriately.

Start by asking an open-ended question like 'How did it go?' Listen hard to the answer which will probably be platitudinous, something like 'Oh fine', 'Yes, it was interesting', or ' Pretty good, really'. Don't accept these as useful enough replies. Follow up immediately with a supplementary question such as 'What was interesting?' or 'What was best?' Listen hard to the answers without interruption. Nod occasionally to encourage them to say more. When you've repeated this sequence and got some specifics out of the person, round off the debriefing session by asking 'So what are you going to do better/differently in future?' Again, refuse to be fobbed off with anything vague and unspecific. Assume that people haven't learned from the experience unless they can look you in the eye and articulate precisely what they are going to carry forward into future actions.

If you get into the habit of instigating debriefing sessions, your people will begin to anticipate the process and be better prepared.

The secret of success is to keep pressing for specifics and to refuse to settle for 'motherhood and apple pie'.

Insisting on debriefs is a straightforward way to help your people learn and develop. The fact that the debriefs also become a conduit to keep you informed is an added bonus.

35 Delegating

Delegating is an essential skill for any manager. By definition you have a job which is more than you can accomplish alone (otherwise you wouldn't be a manager) so you are forced to delegate parts of it to your helpers, ie your subordinates. There is no sensible alternative - even though some managers are reluctant to admit it.

Since you must delegate in order to achieve your job, you might as well do so in a way that provides development opportunities for your delegatees. In a sense this is unavoidable; whenever you delegate you automatically dispense an opportunity to learn. But there are ways of delegating that bump up the learning.

Whenever you delegate you have two separate ingredients to manipulate.

> 1.   The responsibilities, or tasks, you ask someone else to do on your behalf.
>
> 2.   The authority, or powers, you give the delegatee so that they can carry out the responsibilities.

Clearly, the more ambitious you are with the first ingredient, the responsibilities, the greater the potential for development. Ambitiousness has to be judged by taking into account the current skills and abilities of the delegatee. It is entirely possible to delegate inappropriately and set someone too great a challenge. They will still learn from the experience of failing, particularly if you handle it skilfully (see 4, Analysing mistakes), but this is less than satisfactory. It is best to get a match between what someone is currently capable of doing and what you ask them to do. Or, better still, to delegate responsibilities which are a little bit ahead of what the person can currently do; 'stretch' delegation.

When it comes to the second ingredient, authority, the most powerful delegation from a learning and development stand point, means 'letting go' and giving all the authority necessary to complete the job without further referral. This is genuine delegation with a fifty/fifty blending of the two ingredients.

However, there are lesser versions where the amount of authority is reduced and, therefore, no longer commensurate with the delegated responsibilities. Thus you have different strengths of delegation spread along an imaginary continuum. The four main levels of authority are

- just do it
- do it and tell me afterwards
- plan it but check with me before you do it
- consult with me before you plan it.

No matter how much or how little authority you choose to delegate, you remain accountable. Of course, you hope to delegate in such a way that the delegatee *feels* accountable, and *behaves* as if they are accountable, but the buck always stops with you, the delegator. (If you want people to be accountable you have to abandon delegation and go in for job allocation. But that's another story.)

Delegation provides a perfect example of how to twin the demands of getting the job done with the business of providing opportunities for learning and development. The trick is to get double mileage out of something you already have to do.

36 Empowering

Empowerment has been described as delegation for grown-ups (see 35, Delegating) but there is more to it than that. Delegating is something you do to other people whereas empowerment is something people have to do for themselves. Power is what you take, not what you are given. In essence, empowerment happens when individuals take responsibility for their own lives and development. Central to doing so is the issue of choice; the realization that we always have options to choose between. It is never true to say 'there is no alternative'. Of course, there may be some alternatives which are unpalatable or undesirable but there are always plenty of them. It often suits people to assume they have no choice. Choosing involves taking responsibility both for the choice and for its outcomes. The illusion of having no choice is therefore a convenient way to avoid responsibility.

Whilst you cannot empower anyone, other than yourself, there is much that you can do as a manager to create a climate where it is likely your people will get the empowerment message. The more you give your subordinates authority to make decisions and take action, the more likely it is that they will learn how to become empowered. Typical of the lessons they will learn are

-    'I can do it'
-    'I've got nothing to lose'
-    'Nothing ventured, nothing gained'
-    'I make a difference'
-    'I count'
-    'I assume I'm allowed until I'm told otherwise'
-    'I can choose'
-    'There is always an alternative'
-    'I'm in charge of myself'
-    'I can change the way I am'
-    'I'm unique'
-    'I'm responsible'
-    'I decide'.

These lessons are expressed in the first person singular to emphasize the crucial point that ultimately all empowerment is self-empowerment. Many of the sections in this book describe what you as a manager can usefully do to help your people become empowered. Musts are

1,	Acting as a sounding board
6,	Anticipating consequences
22,	Collaborating in decisions
26,	Consulting
35,	Delegating
46,	Giving responsibility for quality
85,	Self-development.

Like it or not, your people are empowered. It is just that you need to help them to realize they are.

37 Enriching jobs

During the Industrial Revolution specializing work was all the rage. Rationally, it was argued, the more specialized the work assigned to an individual, the greater the potential for efficient performance. The snag with this is that the advantages of specializing the work are negated by the disadvantages of having someone do a job they find monotonous and boring. Countless motivation studies demonstrate the importance of work itself as a key determinant of whether someone is switched on or switched off.

From a learning and development standpoint there is no doubt that specialization is a dirty word. The more jobs can be enlarged and enriched the better for both motivation and for development.

There are two main ways to enrich someone's job; you can increase the range of activities (strictly speaking this is called job enlargement) and/or you can increase the level of responsibility. So, for example, you could *enlarge* a subordinate's job by giving them an extra activity such as raising invoices for a new product *in addition* to invoicing for all the existing products. You could *enrich* a subordinate's job by getting them to take responsibility for the accuracy of the invoices they raise. In practice, enlargement and enrichment tend to go hand in hand, but it is possible to do one without the other.

Involving the job holder in thoughts on how their job could be enlarged and enriched is in itself an example of job enlargement. The secret of success is to ensure that the different aspects of the work someone has to do are related, rather than being a hotch potch of miscellaneous things. One way to assess this is to check whether the knowledge and skills necessary to perform the work are closely allied and can reasonably be possessed by the same person. It would be reasonable, therefore, to enrich a salesperson's job by increasing the range of products or type of customers, but unreasonable to expect the salesperson to take on responsibility for psychometric testing.

Broadening the range of activities and increasing the amount of responsibility automatically generates learning opportunities for the job holder. This is so even if the enrichment is temporary, as in covering for holidays (27, Covering for holidays) or 'acting up'.

38 Experimenting

If we don't experiment we drastically reduce opportunities to learn and find new ways to do business. Experiments can be foolhardy, where the stakes are too high and the risks too great. Chernobyl springs to mind where departing from regulations and experimenting caused an uncontrollable series of catastrophic events at the nuclear power station. All experiments increase the unknowns, and therefore the risks, but as with most things in life there is a time to experiment and learn from so doing, and a time to be cautious and stick to the tried and tested.

From a learning and development point of view, experimenting is to be applauded. Learning is seriously limited if you and your people minimize uncertainty and risk and stick to what is safe. The idea is to experiment, not for its own sake, but in order to make discoveries about best practice that would otherwise be unobtainable. The best way to encourage experimentation is to become a role model and be seen to be doing it yourself. The sorts of experiments you could conduct will clearly depend on your specific circumstances and the nature of your work, but here are some suggestions to whet your appetite

- experiment with different start times for meetings

- experiment by having standing-only meetings (or lying-down meetings)

- experiment with a fifteen minute cat-nap straight after lunch

- experiment by ignoring all in-coming mail and seeing if and when anyone asks for a response

- experiment with fixed periods during the day when you are unavailable, your door is closed

- experiment with the rule that you will only handle a given piece of paper once

- experiment by delegating unusual things to the people who least expect it

- experiment with telling your boss you don't know the answer/you can't get something done 'by yesterday'/you are going home on time/you have made a mistake/you want his/her help

- experiment with having no office, no desk, no secretary, no telephone

- experiment by having an hour each day when you wander around talking to people

- experiment by visiting an 'unknown' part of your organization each week

- experiment by travelling to work a different way

- experiment by being polite to someone you are usually rude to and being blunt to someone you are usually 'diplomatic' with

- experiment with a different diary system

- experiment by being inconsistent and 'moving the goal posts'

- experiment by volunteering to do something you've never taken on before

- experiment by being informal in formal situations and formal in informal situations

- experiment by writing down six options then roll a dice and do the one that comes up

- experiment by reading a different daily newspaper or a different trade journal or a different type of book

- experiment by being spontaneous in a situation where you'd normally prepare carefully and by preparing carefully for a situation where you'd normally 'play it by ear'.

You may think some of these suggestions a little zany, but most of them are unlikely to cause offence or create mayhem. All require a little courage because they take you out of your 'comfort zone' and you aren't sure how they will turn out. That is the whole point of an experiment, to try something out in order to make discoveries.

Once you've launched yourself as an experimenter it is easy to encourage your people to indulge. Make sure you reinforce their bravery with lashings of support and always ask them what they've learned from the experiment.

39 External consultants

The involvement of external consultants is often resented by staff because the consultants are perceived as

- aliens who attempt to force-fit a solution regardless of its appropriateness to the 'culture' of the organization

- auditors who have come to check up on performance and find it wanting

- performers who sweep in with lots of hype and clear off just when the going gets tough

- parasites who are paid vast fees for recommending what people inside the organization (prophets in their own country) have been advocating for years.

Despite these jaundiced and, it has to be admitted, sometimes justified perceptions, there is much your staff can learn from watching and working with external consultants.

Clearly learning is massively increased if your staff have the opportunity to work alongside the consultants. Some of the best consultants seek to establish a partnership with their clients and are quite brazen about their own learning from collaborative ventures. They know that the project is more likely to be successful, *and* that they stand to learn more, from the synergy that results from a cocktail of external and internal expertise.

What might your staff learn from involvement with external consultants? Here are some possibilities

- how to establish rapport and gain the trust and co-operation of strangers who are initially wary and/or hostile

- how to negotiate an unambiguous contract with clear objectives and terms of reference

- how to see beyond the presenting problem, gather

data and do a thorough diagnosis

- how to surface people's concerns and reservations

- when to behave as a high profile 'expert' and when to behave as a low profile facilitator

- how to remain client focused and check needs are being met/exceeded

- how to influence with no 'clout' or direct power to make changes or implement anything

- how to feedback recommendations in a way that maximizes the chances of getting acceptance and action

- how to handle passive and active resistance

- when to call it a day and walk away.

In addition to these behavioural/process lessons there are likely to be many others generated by the problem the consultants are helping with. Perhaps they are experts in their field and each interaction is the equivalent of a mini-tutorial. Perhaps as outsiders, with experience in a range of other organizations, they can broaden the perspective of your subordinates and help them to be less insular. If the external consultants perform poorly, thus confirming your subordinates' worst fears, there is still much to learn. Get your subordinates to identify mistakes made by the consultants and suggest how these could have been avoided or the damage repaired. You could even get your subordinates to write a report with recommendations and send it to the consultants thus giving them a taste of their own medicine.

40 Flip-charting

Getting someone to write on a flip chart or white board may seem a triviality but there are some useful lessons to learn from this, amongst them being

- listening to what other people say without interruption

- recording verbatim the essence of what someone says

- asking questions of clarification to check that what has been recorded is correct

- overcoming feelings of shame and embarrassment when not knowing how to spell certain words

- overcoming reluctance to stand up and undertake such a high profile 'public' role

- resisting the temptation to act as a censor and only recording what he/she supports (the power of the pen)

- writing fast but legibly.

You should certainly have a flip chart or white board in your office and wherever you hold regular meetings. They are a 'must' for objective setting, agenda setting, recording ideas, reviewing what went well and what could have gone better and so on. The effectiveness of all discussions and meetings is enhanced if a flip chart is used to record salient points that are visible to all the participants. If need be, relevant flip charts can be typed up or photocopied and circulated after the discussion. This is far more efficient than having someone take clandestine minutes that no-one can see until it is too late.

The best way to use flip charting as a learning opportunity is to rotate the task so that over a period of time all your subordinates have a go. Of course, some will do the job better than others but then you will use it as an opportunity to coach (see 21, Coaching).

41 Forecasting

All forecasting is brave because the chances of being proved wrong are so high. Forecasts are an extrapolation of past trends and present facts plus large dollops of guesswork about how things will turn out in the future. The further ahead you go, the more the unknowns and the more you have to base your forecast on assumptions. The whole thing is most unnerving. As someone once remarked, 'forecasting is like driving a car when you can only see through the rear window'.

Forecasting, like planning (see 69, Planning and 6, Anticipating consequences) is an activity which generates lots of learning. For example, when forecasting people are likely to learn

- to avoid quick fixes by having a future focus and 'managing the present from the future'

- the difference between assumptions and facts

- how to put current activities into a longer term perspective

- the importance of breaking free of 'mind sets' and challenging paradigms

- how to handle the uncertainty and ambiguity of not knowing

- how the future is not merely an extension of the past

- the difference between incremental changes (ie step by step modifications of the present) and transformational change (ie unexpected quantum leaps)

- how changes can start as predictable incremental steps but suddenly flip and become transformational.

You can give your subordinates opportunities to forecast without it necessarily being part of any grandiose strategic planning activity. For example, whenever you ask a subordinate to set an objective, whether it be for the short, medium or long term, you are inviting them to forecast. All objectives, without exception, are an attempt to describe a state of affairs that will exist at some point in the future. Everyone has to set objectives and so everyone needs to be a forecaster. Start by getting your subordinates to set short term objectives where the crystal ball gazing element is minimal. Then gradually involve them in setting longer term objectives where the uncertainties are greater.

In addition to objective setting, there are plenty of other opportunities to get your subordinates to stick their necks out and do some forecasting. Furnish them with the relevant data and invite them to forecast the month's production figures, the quarterly sales figures, the company's annual turnover, customer attrition. Anything that can be measured lends itself to some forecasting and it's all good practice at wrestling with the skills involved. You could even offer a small prize for the person whose forecast turns out to be the most accurate.

42 Funding development

Most of the ideas in this book cost no money at all. Learning and development is simply piggybacked on things which have to happen for other reasons. This entry is different because it will cost you. The idea is to give all your subordinates an annual development budget. The money must be spent on self-development and, if you wish, you could spell out other guidelines and constraints to do with the relevance and appropriateness of the learning to the subordinate's current job. The fewer constraints the better however, except that subsequently every one must 'justify' their expenditure and spell out what they have learned.

The level of funding obviously depends on what can be made available and the number of subordinates you have. It could be as small as £200 per person but preferably would be closer to £1000. If you wish, the self-development fund could accumulate as a result of savings made elsewhere. It would act as an incentive to cut costs if people knew that they would directly benefit from the savings made.

The ideas people have for self-development will obviously be many and varied. Some examples might be

- hiring or making audio or video tapes
- covering expenses incurred in conducting a survey or investigation
- paying an outside speaker's fees
- going on a course or seminar
- funding a project
- purchasing books, magazines or newspapers
- photocopying costs
- paying a consultant's fees
- reimbursing travelling expenses when going to schools or other local institutions to give talks etc.

Whatever the expenditure, it is important that each budget holder is called to account just as any other budget holder would be. Have periodic reviews where people report what they have spent on what activities and the self-development gains they have made. It would be better still if you joined in this process as a fully-fledged self-development budget holder. Since all development is self-development it would be paradoxical not to start with yourself.

43 Giving Feedback

Feedback is absolutely essential for learning and development and yet in the majority of workplaces people do not get enough. People at work have three basic rights which can only be met by receiving ongoing feedback

- to know what is expected of them
- to know how they are doing
- to know what they need to do to improve/become even better.

Interestingly, most people for most of the time are lucky if one or two of these rights are met, let alone all three.

You may be amongst the many managers who are reluctant to give feedback, but if you withhold it you are failing in one of the most fundamental duties of any manager. It is impossible to provide for the three basic rights without giving feedback. People who are deprived of feedback from their manager compensate in two potentially dangerous ways. Firstly, they start to rely exclusively on scraps of feedback from other people, colleagues, friends, customers, anyone who will offer it. This in itself is no bad thing except that feedback from these sources may be at variance with your own perceptions. In the absence of your feedback, subordinates will understandably become dependent on what you might regard as spurious data. Secondly, and even worse, people deprived of feedback fill the void by giving themselves feedback and assuming, in the absence of any contrary indicators, that all is well. The longer this goes on, the more difficult it becomes to grasp the nettle and, when you do, the more traumatic the discovery that your perceptions differ from theirs.

So, the provision of feedback is a non-negotiable, bottom-line requirement *if* you are to help your people to learn and develop. Always remember, however, that the receiver of the feedback has the right to decide whether or not to act on it. Having listened and understood, the receiver is always the final arbiter in deciding what to accept and what to reject. The choice is theirs. If you withhold feedback you have deprived them of the right to decide and therefore of one of the most powerful learning opportunities of all.

Feedback can, of course, be positive or negative. For more on the skills required see 70, Praising and 30, Criticizing. For advice on how to become the receiver, rather than the provider, of feedback see 95, Upward appraisal/feedback.

44 Giving itemized responses

An itemized response is the rather unattractive name given to a specific technique that forces people to consider the merits of an idea before being allowed to state a concern. The technique is part of a creative thinking approach similar to Brainstorming (see section 13), known as synectics.

At a stroke, the imposition of itemized responses swings the balance in a discussion or meeting from negative to positive. This is how it works. The educational system ensures that people are trained better to analyse than to synthesize. Analysing involves taking ideas to bits and critically examining the individual parts. Synthesising means putting different ideas together in such a way that something is added. The result is greater than the sum of the individual parts. The trouble with too much analysis is that it concentrates on finding fault with ideas and nothing gets done. The expressions 'analysing to death' and 'analysis to paralysis' sum up the dangers perfectly.

Itemized responses reverse the over-analytical tendencies by insisting that everyone must say three things they like about an idea before being permitted to state one concern. The ratio of three to one is deliberate to emphasize the positive over the negative. Even the concern has to be posed as an open-ended question starting with the words 'how to...' (eg How to get people to buy into the idea? How to make the idea cost effective? How to make the idea practical/feasible?). This is a more positive way to state a concern than a bald statement rubbishing the idea.

The insistence on itemized responses is never exactly popular but in addition to forcing people to be more positive it generates a number of useful lessons - especially useful for people who tend to be too analytical for their own good.

Valuable lessons learned include

- the realization that *all* ideas, whilst not perfect, have merit

- the importance of listening hard to someone else's idea whilst temporarily suspending judgement

- how it is possible to say three different 'good' things about an idea even though initially the idea was rejected

- how each 'good' thing which is said about an idea has the potential to spawn further ideas and/or to improve the original idea

- how the way concerns are expressed (ie as questions, not as statements) makes a profound difference to people's responses; they are much more likely to search for ways to overcome the concern (ie to find answers to the question posed) than to join in the clamour to have the idea killed off

- the realization that you don't require much of a brain to come up with reasons not to do things and that all ideas pass through a stage where they can easily be rubbished

- the surprising discovery that people's behaviour can be changed by the imposition of a simple rule and that changed behaviour causes changed thinking and attitudes, rather than the other way round.

Itemized responses can be imposed on any discussion or meeting that is getting bogged down by negative behaviour. The swing of the pendulum to positive behaviour is instant and dramatic with the added advantage that much is learned from the struggle to fight against the tendency to be too analytical.

45 Giving outside talks

Any form of public speaking (see 71, Presenting) provides a rich array of learning opportunities, not least because so many people are irrationally terrified by it. Fascinatingly, many years after a public speaking *faux pas* the memory lingers as vividly as if it were yesterday. Public speaking is clearly an emotional learning experience where much is at stake for the speaker, though rarely for the audience.

If you have subordinates who would benefit from some public speaking and are wary of doing it, starting them off with talks outside the organization is a kinder way to provide them with their first opportunities. It may sound callous, but should things go wrong, it is easier to make a fool of yourself in front of strangers, who will never have to be seen again, than with bosses, colleagues and other people within the organization who have to be lived with afterwards. Let your people cut their teeth on expendable strangers.

Invitations from outside bodies such as local schools, colleges, and voluntary organizations either arrive in the normal course of events or can easily be engineered. Many clubs and societies are only too pleased to have a willing volunteer to help fill their calendar of events almost irrespective of the topic.

What lessons, in addition to those given in 71, Presenting, might your people learn from giving outside talks?

-       the importance of doing some 'research' to establish the size and type of audience, the level at which to pitch the talk and how best to get on the audience's 'wave length'

-       how much your people really know about the business. This often only becomes apparent when they realize that all the things they take for granted are new, perhaps even astonishing, to an outside audience

-       how to establish rapport with a room full of strangers and with audience mixes which differ significantly from the people normally encountered at work

- how interested lay people are in what your business does, how it works, how it is organized, what its values are

- how much easier it is to feel genuine pride for your organization's achievements when they are described to an outside audience

- the importance of keeping in touch with members of the public, to understand their concerns about employment issues, the environment, the links between the worlds of education and work and so on.

These are lessons it is easy for you to provide at minimal risk. Outside bodies will be pleased to have speakers and your people's confidence will be boosted by the kudos of being asked to represent the organization. It's a win-win with valuable learning thrown in free.

46 Giving responsibility for quality

The drive for quality is, as everyone knows by now, a whole philosophy or 'way of life'. The quest for zero defects, getting things right first time and prevention rather than correction is all part of the process of total quality management. The quality gurus such as Deming and Crosby have helped to put continuous improvement at the top of the conscious agenda in many organizations.

It is impossible to achieve total quality unless you make each of your subordinates responsible for the quality of their own work. By definition the only person who can get it right first time is the person who actually does the job. By the time poor quality work reaches you it becomes, at best, a case of 'right second time' and that is expensive in time, money and frustration.

Delegating responsibility for quality is not only essential from a quality point of view, it also massively increases learning opportunities. Indeed, the philosophy of continuous improvement and learning and development are inextricably intertwined; you can't have one without the other.

The problem, as with all delegation (see 35, Delegating), is how to solve the paradox of, on the one hand, 'letting go' so that your subordinates have responsibility with commensurate authority and, on the other hand, remaining accountable for something as vital as quality. The answer is to break with the usual tradition of delegating the 'whats' and leaving the 'hows' for the delegatee to decide. Time and time again recurring quality problems have been shown to result from inadequate systems and processes rather than from inadequate human beings. The processes hold the key. If you focus solely on the ends, the outputs, and relinquish your interest in the means, the 'hows', then you will miss the essence of quality management and fail to solve the paradox.

So giving responsibility for quality means *never* saying 'I don't want to know how you do it; just do it'. You must always be intensely interested in the 'hows', not because you don't trust people, and not because you are going to do it yourself, but because the means are what quality management is all about. When delegating responsibility for quality, therefore, you need to do the following

- describe the responsibilities (ie tasks/activities, the 'whats') being delegated

- agree the quality standards that apply

- explore how the standards will be met, the process and resources required

- agree the authority the delegatee needs to implement the 'hows'

- review, with whatever frequency was agreed, the quality standards and the processes, *and improve them.*

This is an iterative process because one review cascades into the next and so on for ever.

The learning mileage in all this is considerable. Firstly, there is the whole business of articulating and agreeing precise enough quality standards. Secondly, the exploration of how the standards will be met. Thirdly, the reviews. And this only includes what your subordinates will learn from the parts in the process that directly involve you. In addition, there are the numerous lessons to be learned from the day-to-day challenge of 'doing it right first time'. It's almost a case of 'never mind the quality; feel the learning!'

47 Griping sessions

Strong feelings of dissatisfaction with the way things are create a prelude to change. By contrast, feelings of satisfaction and complacency are a recipe for a continuation of the *status quo*. You need, therefore, to whip up dissatisfaction in your people and an excellent way to do this is to hold gripe sessions. A gripe session is an invitation for people to complain and grumble *ad nauseam*.

Now you might think it crazy to give specific air time to your people's gripes but, handled properly, they make a valuable contribution to the change process and generate learning opportunities for all concerned. This is how it works. Firstly, a formula

$$D \times V \times F > R$$

where:

> D = dissatisfaction with the current reality
> V = vision of how much better things could be
> F = first steps to begin to close the gap between D and V
> > = greater than
> R = resistance

Notice that the whole process starts with dissatisfaction. Grumbles on their own might be depressing and de-motivating but grumbles, coupled with a vision of how much better things could be, create a positive 'tension for change'. The desire to close the gap generates the first steps and, hey presto, people are raring to go.

If you hold a gripe session with complacent people, you need to take the lead in challenging the *status quo* and stirring things up (see 18, Challenging). The more dissatisfaction you can create the better. Each gripe provides the spark for visions of a preferred future. A preferred future is truly visionary, a conceptual leap that breaks free of existing paradigms and transcends current constraints and practicalities. By contrast, a predictive future is less visionary and a mere extension of what happens now.

The lessons learned by your people when you involve them in this

change process are likely to include

- an appreciation of how essential it is to be assertive when expressing current dissatisfactions and 'tell it the way it really is'. No complain, no gain

- how to convert dissatisfactions into visions describing a preferred future (and the difference between a preferred future and a predictive future)

- the difference between incremental and transformational change (the former, step-by-step modifications to the present situation; the latter, where extensions to the present are no longer appropriate and things need to be 'transformed')

- how even transformational changes start with some small, incremental steps. 'A walk of a thousand miles, starts with but one step'

- how resistance crumbles once people are involved in the D, V and F part of the change formula.

If you handle the gripe sessions well, your subordinates will also learn that you want to hear their dissatisfactions and can do so without becoming defensive or 'shooting the messenger'.

48 Holding a promises auction or swop shop

Here is an idea loosely based on a fund-raising ploy sometimes used by voluntary organizations to raise money for good causes. At a promises auction pledges from people to provide certain skills and services are auctioned instead of the tangible goods you find at a conventional auction. Promises range from babysitting and cooking to decorating and ironing. Instead of having a promises auction where the pledges are social and domestic, why not have one where people promise to swop work skills and know-how?

People always have pieces of expertise that they themselves take for granted and that others could benefit from. In the normal course of events there is no mechanism to pass on these skills to colleagues. A promises auction or swop shop corrects the situation by providing an opportunity for people to 'advertise' skills they are willing to exchange for other skills. Typical examples might be promises to

- teach how to use a word processor

- show how to use, and do simple trouble shooting on, a photocopying machine

- explain how E mail works

- pass on project management skills

- show how statistical process control works

- show how to read a balance sheet or do double entry book-keeping

- show how to use an overhead projector

- show how the stock control system works

- explain the organization chart

- explain what the personnel department does, or the intricacies of certain personnel policies and procedures.

Once people get the idea, many promises will be forthcoming depending on the nature of the work in your department.

It is best to give people lots of notice and a deadline by when they need to submit their promise. The promises can either be displayed on a notice board or, better still, a mock auction can be held where each promise is given a lot number and goes under the hammer just like the real thing. Purchasers can either use tokens, or swop promise for promise or, if you like, use real money to raise funds for a good cause.

The main point, however, is to use the auction as a device to promote a small learning community amongst your subordinates. If you held a promises auction, say, no more than twice a year it would keep the idea sufficiently novel and fresh and you would be unlikely to run out of skills and expertise that people are willing to exchange.

49 Identifying 'stoppers' and blockages

Despite your best efforts (see 36, Empowering), people are often reluctant to take initiatives for fear of retribution. All initiatives spring from a combination of three factors; people have to feel

- able
- willing
- and allowed.

Sometimes people don't do things because, even though they are able and allowed, they are unwilling. At other times people are willing but handicapped by a lack of ability. Perhaps the most wasteful permutation is when people are perfectly able and willing but do not feel they are allowed, ie don't have the necessary authority to go ahead and do it.

It's your task as a manager constantly to ensure that your people are able, willing *and* allowed by identifying what stops them from doing what you want them to do and removing the impediments and blockages. Often 'stoppers' are more in the mind than real and frequently it is the imaginary ones that do the most damage and are easiest to sweep away.

Here is a simple routine for identifying the factors that prevent people from taking the initiatives you long for.

1. Ask people what it is their customers expect (ie *anyone,* internal or external, to whom they provide goods and/or services).

2. Ask people what it is they should do to *exceed* their customers' expectations (ie to delight their customers, not merely to satisfy them).

3. Ask people what stops them from exceeding their customers' expectations. Stoppers can be anything from poor resources to lack of time, from unreliable equipment to lack of authority.

4. Finally, ask people what they need to remove the stoppers. Welcome all feasible ideas.

You may not in all cases be able, willing or allowed to provide what your people claim to need but at least you have surfaced their perceptions and this gives you the raw material you need to make progress.

From a learning point of view this process helps people in a number of ways. Firstly, they learn to be customer-focused in all they do. Secondly, they learn that merely to meet customers' expectations is not enough; consistently exceeding them is what customer service is all about. Thirdly, they learn that it is up to them to identify the 'stoppers', to alert you, their manager, and to have ideas to improve the situation. Finally, and perhaps most importantly, they learn to take initiatives and that 'it is easier to ask for forgiveness than for permission'.

They might even learn that you are there to help them and ease the way to quality performance rather than to interfere inappropriately and cramp their style.

50 Inducting new-starters

Each time a new member of staff joins you, whether on a temporary or permanent basis, it creates a splendid learning opportunity. Obviously the new-starter has much to learn but, with a little ingenuity, you can also make it a developmental opportunity for other people.

Induction is important because, as the old maxim goes, you never get a second chance to make a first impression. It *is* possible to recover from a bad start, but it is easier not to have to. The new-starter's first impressions are unique and have a lasting impact on his or her subsequent performance and morale. In fact, a major peril with all new-starters is that they arrive with unrealistic expectations and, if the induction process isn't handled properly, come down to earth with a nasty bump. The danger of disillusion and, worse still, apathy are very real.

The best way to approach induction is to regard it as a process and not merely as a course where the new-starter needs to be told certain things. Treat induction as a mini-project that, like all projects, needs to be managed. The initial objective is to enable the new-starter to be productive as soon as possible. Depending on the complexities of the work content, this might be achieved in the space of a few hours or a few days. The longer term objective is fully to integrate the new-starter into the organization, its culture and ways and means, so that he/she understands the context in which their work is carried out and can make a wider contribution.

A novel way to maximize learning from the induction process is to set the new-starter the challenge of master-minding their own induction programme on an investigative basis. All you need to do is draw up a list of questions for the new-starter to answer and recommend some useful contacts, sources and resources. Typical questions might include

- how do you see your responsibilities and what authority will you need to carry them out?

- what is the company's policy on pay and conditions, holiday entitlement, sick pay, overtime, safety, etc, etc?

- what expectations do the following have of you

    - your boss
    - your subordinates
    - your colleagues
    - your customers?

- how would you describe the organization's philosophy, values, mission, strategic objectives?

If you tackle induction on this do-it-yourself basis it is vital to hold regular reviews with the new-starter to establish how he/she is getting on, discover what he/she is learning and give reassurance and guidance.

It is also helpful to provide each new-starter with a designated colleague who can act as a 'minder', confidant and guide. This gives the minder an opportunity to learn as they wrestle with all the queries, point the new-starter in the right direction and have fresh perspectives on what has become a familiar *status quo*. If the minder is smart he/she will also learn how to support and reassure the new-starter as they go through the psychological process of adjusting their expectations to match the reality of the situation. New-starters have the potential to raise the awareness of everyone they encounter in those precious first few hours or days.

51 Interviewing

Interviews are a structured way to find out as much as possible about someone in a short time. Sorting out the objectives for the interview, how best to structure it and the questions to ask is always a fascinating business from which there is much to learn. Of course, interviews are conducted for a variety of purposes, not least as a notoriously unreliable selection technique, but here we are solely concerned with interviews as learning devices.

You can easily create opportunities for members of your staff to conduct interviews from which they will learn. Here are some possibilities. Invite your staff to interview

- each other to find out about interests, skills, what makes them tick, opinions about recent events, etc.

- you to discover your management 'philosophy', values and standards

- your boss to quiz him/her on where the organization is going, visions for the future, etc.

- people in other parts of your organization to find out what they do

- customers to find out their perceptions of the service you provide and what their expectations are

- competitors to compare and contrast best practices

- outside 'speakers' to find out about a variety of topics (the speakers are invited to subject themselves to the scrutiny of the interviewers rather than to come with a prepared spiel).

Always insist that the interviews are organized and purposeful with nothing left to chance. As much of the learning flows from the preparatory activities as from the conduct of the interview itself. Also give a time slot into which the interview must fit; forty-five minutes is about right unless it is going to go into extraordinary depths, in which case an hour should be sufficient.

Finally, after the interview ensure that the interviewer(s) review what they learned from the experience of planning and conducting an interview and from the topics explored.

Likely lessons include

- how to set realistic objectives

- how to phrase initial and supplementary questions to find out what you want to know

- how to listen and understand

- how much can be discovered in a short time

- how willing, forthcoming and expansive most people are if you put them at their ease

- how much more can be learned by being proactive and taking charge of the process rather than passively waiting to be spoon-fed what someone else decides you should know.

And, in addition to these lessons learned, add the information gained from the contents of the interview. So, instead of constantly explaining, briefing and exhorting, put the boot on the other foot and give your subordinates the opportunity to find out for themselves. They'll relish the prospect and the messages will stick.

52 Job descriptions

Job descriptions are rather out of vogue at present as organizations seek to find ways to be more flexible and more responsive to their customers. The complaint has always been that attempts to specify a job in writing is a recipe for unnecessary rigidity and invariably fails to capture the essence and true spirit of the job itself. Cynics would say that the sentence '... and does other duties as required' covers a multitude of sins and is probably the only accurate statement in the whole description.

Of course, it is true that jobs evolve and are dynamic and that sticking to the letter of a job description would be ridiculously restrictive, but that only argues for frequently updating job descriptions rather than having none at all. The advantage of job descriptions is that they clarify the main duties of a job holder and in doing so reduce misconceptions and misunderstandings. Everyone has a basic right to know what is expected of them and job descriptions, whilst not the whole answer, are a useful starting point.

The best way to get learning mileage out of job descriptions is to ask each of your people to write their own and then to go through the process of agreeing it with you and/or colleagues and/or subordinates. No-one should ever have their job description written for them by someone else. To do so deprives them of a valuable learning opportunity. The act of describing, in fairly precise terms, your key objectives and responsibilities is a worthwhile discipline in its own right as well as providing an explicit check that what people *think* they are supposed to do more or less matches the expectations of other interested parties.

It is best to adopt a standardized format for job descriptions. The description should include the overall purpose of the job and principle duties or tasks which constitute the job. If you regard the job description merely as a starting point, and not a definitive document, it can be kept simple and straightforward. Other important aspects are best clarified by discussion and agreement, things such as specific objectives nested within the overall job purpose, priorities, and levels of authority needed to carry out those duties.

The learning flows from a combination of compiling the initial job description and, more importantly, the ensuing discussions that add finishing touches and lead to unambiguous job clarification. Job descriptions thus become a means to an end, not an end in themselves.

Jobs, of course, are dynamic so job descriptions must not become static and out of date. The whole process of description and clarification bears repetition and is not a one-off exercise.

53 Keeping activity/time logs

Time, as everyone knows, is a vital resource which is completely inelastic. Come what may, we all have twenty-four hours in a day. Strictly speaking it is impossible to *make* extra time, only to free up time by rearranging what we do with the time we've got. A lack of time is the most common excuse for not doing something that we don't really want to do. Helping your people to manage their time more efficiently directly contributes to their effectiveness and, therefore, to yours. It generates some lessons learned which are so fundamental that they have the capacity permanently to affect a person's whole philosophy of life.

You have to help your subordinates discover how they now use their time before anything can be done to improve it. Most people are only vaguely aware of how much time they spend on different activities and, until clear patterns are established, it is impossible to identify where savings can be made. Collecting accurate data is the key to the whole exercise and a learning experience in its own right.

Encourage your subordinates to keep detailed notes of the time they spend on different activities for a minimum of two and preferably for four weeks. The weeks need not be consecutive but they do need to be typical or representative of what happens normally. Expect resistance to the idea of keeping a time log. To people who are already feeling under time pressure, the additional chore of keeping a log will seem like the straw that broke the camel's back. Insist that viable solutions to their problems can only emerge from an analysis of where their time goes at present.

There are two schools of thought about the format of time logs. Either you start with blank sheets of paper and every fifteen minutes describe activities undertaken, or you use a category system by listing in advance main activities and each hour note how many minutes have been spent on each. It is vital to include space for 'other activities' to cover miscellaneous things that won't have been thought of in advance. If in doubt about the categories, it is best to phase the two approaches by using the blank sheet method for the first two weeks and analysing it to discover the categories against which you note times for the second two weeks. Whichever method you encourage your subordinates to adopt, keep it simple so that data collection is sustainable through thick and thin for the required period.

When the logs have been completed ask your subordinates for their conclusions and proposals for improved time management. Refuse to be fobbed off with excuses or vagueness. Keep challenging (see 18, Challenging) until you are satisfied it makes sense.

Lessons learned from keeping and analysing time logs are likely to include such fundamental things as

- the balance between proactive and reactive time

- the amount of discretionary time (always more than people realize)

- the distinction between what is important and what is urgent and the whole business of prioritizing

- the time wasters (ie procrastination, being a perfectionist, untidiness, interruptions, rambling meetings and so on)

- the importance of saying no assertively

- the importance of sound, repeatable systems for all routine activities

- the need to balance conflicting demands from home and work

- the supreme importance of 'now' (life is just one now after another)

- the usefulness of frequently asking yourself the question 'is what I am doing right now the best way to spend my time?'

These insights, if you'll forgive the pun, are timeless. Once the lessons of self-management have been learned, they literally become a way of life. Helping your subordinates to acquire such fundamental wisdom will transform them, you and the business.

54 Keeping learning logs

Here is an idea to increase learning from any activity, big or small. Most people are subliminal learners from experience; they learn but are not sure what or how. This means they are unable to communicate what they have learned to others and are severely handicapped at practising continuous improvement and development. The answer is to help people to supplement what they learn intuitively by getting them to adopt a discipline that makes their learning more explicit. Learning logs are one way to bring this about.

A learning log is a simple way to record notes about an experience at work (or elsewhere come to that), the conclusions that have been reached and a plan to do something better/differently. The precise format can vary providing it is structured to elicit these three pieces of information; the experience, the conclusions, the plan. If people have an aversion to writing things down, they can talk into a dictaphone and have it typed out at a later stage.

The simple act of writing or talking about an experience, and what has been learned from it, converts people from tacit to explicit learners and that is what the learning log routine is designed to do. The frequency of learning log entries is discretionary. It might be once per day or once per week. Whatever happens do not allow learning logs to be reserved for only the most striking or dramatic experiences. To do so misses out on the more mundane experiences, ie everyday happenings and incidents, all of which have developmental potential if only they were consciously trawled for learning.

Lessons learned from keeping learning logs are likely to include

- the worthwhileness of pondering experiences instead of just rushing headlong to the next one

- the importance of making considered judgements rather than jumping to conclusions

- how vital it is to do something better or differently in the light of conclusions (otherwise what is the point of having them?)

-   an understanding of the iterative process of a plan to do something better or differently becoming, when it is implemented, an experience in its own right that lends itself to reviewing, concluding and planning

-   that the experience - review - conclude - plan cycle is the essence of continuous improvement and development.

You can lend support to the learning log discipline by keeping a log yourself and by talking to people about what they have learned (see 78, Reviewing learning). This adds credence to the whole thing and, if people know you are going to review their learning log entries, makes it more likely they will do it.

55 Learning contracts

A learning contract is a formal agreement, in writing, between you and a subordinate spelling out what he/she will learn in a specified period and how it will be assessed. The strength of a learning contract lies in its formality, thus making the requirement to learn and develop explicit and imposing the rolling discipline of negotiating a new contract when the time limit for the old one expires.

Whilst a learning contract is formal and in writing, it need not be complex and certainly requires nothing in the way of small print. One side of an A4 page is ample, with space for the learning objective, the proposed activities, the resources needed, the means of assessment and the target date. It is difficult to give specific examples of the contents of a learning contract because the whole point is that it is tailor-made to the needs and opportunities of the individual. Typically, however, contracts cover gains in knowledge, techniques and skills to improve the person's job performance. Examples might be

> to acquire more knowledge about
>
> - information technology
> - financial analysis
> - market segmentation.
>
> to become more skilled at
>
> - negotiating
> - presenting
> - communicating in a foreign language.

The possibilities are endless and many of the ideas in this book could be incorporated into learning contracts. It is a good idea to aim for incremental contracts where knowledge and/or skills are acquired in attainable steps or stages over, say, six to eight week time spans. Setting grandiose objectives which are long term and ambitious is too daunting and means that the contracting process is engaged in too infrequently. Six contracting sessions per year for each of your direct reports would be an admirable habit to adopt.

Learning contracts are attractive because they

- are individually oriented/tailor-made

- pinpoint specific knowledge/skill areas to help the individual improve,or become better at, his/her job performance

- are appropriate for anybody irrespective of function, seniority or age

- build in the need for learning to be assessed bi-monthly when the next contract is negotiated

- encourage people to make and take work-based learning opportunities

- 'force' you and your subordinates to have purposeful interactions about learning that you probably wouldn't have without the discipline of learning contracts.

If you want further advice and guidance on learning contracts, read 'The Management Learning Contract Manual' which is Part 2 in a book by George Boak called 'Developing Managerial Competences' published by Pitmans, ISBN 0-273-03326-3. The examples are all managerial but the principles extend to all categories of staff.

56 Learning from in-trays

Sometimes, at assessment centres and on management courses, you will encounter an in-tray exercise where decisions have to be made about how best to deal with the contents of an imaginary in-tray. To add spice to the exercise there is usually a scenario that imposes a tight deadline by when all the decisions must have been made, and your impending absence from the office for an overseas trip during which time you must ensure things get done.

Just think what people could learn from the contents of your *real* in-tray. There is no need to contrive anything; as you know only too well, it already exists. It is just a question of working out how to use your in-tray as a learning opportunity for your subordinates. Here are two different ways of doing this

1. You could invite a subordinate (a different one each time) to come and sit beside you while you do your in-tray. It would be necessary to give a running commentary as you work through the contents so that the subordinate could listen to your prioritising, decision-making and rationale.

2. You could hand over your in-tray to a subordinate, who would decide how to process the contents and then justify his/her decisions with you. It would be useful to give minimal guidance by, for example, asking him/her to sort the contents into three categories; do, delegate and defer. You could either busy yourself with something else while the subordinate 'does' your in-tray or sit and coach them through it (see 21, Coaching).

If you consider the contents of your own in-tray too sensitive or confidential to lend themselves to this sort of public scrutiny you could still salvage something from the idea by occasionally getting two of your subordinates to swop their in-trays and see what they can learn from each other. At the very least this would give them some understanding of, maybe even empathy with, each other's problems.

In-trays are yet another example of a ready-made activity with the potential to generate learning and development. There are lessons to do with prioritising, decision-making and delegating as well as subordinates gaining considerable insight into the range and variety of things that managers have to deal with. Not only that, but you'd get your in-tray done as well!

57 Listening

Listening is one of the key skills involved in the acquisition of knowledge but unfortunately many people are bad listeners and this considerably hampers their learning and development. Bad listeners are easy to spot. They frequently

- interrupt
- misinterpret what was said
- hear what they expect to hear rather than what was actually said
- look bored and uninterested
- talk nineteen to the dozen
- look impatient or distracted
- do other things while claiming to be listening
- think what to say next rather than listening to what is being said
- can't paraphrase or 'read back' accurately what someone else said.

There are a number of ways you can use to force people to develop their listening skills. The simplest is to impose spot checks by asking someone without warning to paraphrase what has just been said (see 93, Testing understanding). The threat of being called upon to paraphrase concentrates the mind wonderfully. A more considerable challenge is to give a poor listener the job of recording things on a flip-chart or white board (see 40, Flip-charting). Insisting on itemized responses (see 44, Giving itemized responses) is another no-nonsense way of getting people to listen hard.

Perhaps the most ruthless way to improve listening skills is to play the wallflower game. You can adapt this to suit your purposes and time scales but typically you go through the following routine.

- Invite a bad listener to describe to a small group of colleagues a current problem or concern he/she would like some advice on. Allow only a maximum of five minutes to brief the group.

- Ban the bad listener from saying anything else for twenty to thirty minutes while the group discusses his/her problem. The bad listener has to 'sit out' (like a wallflower at a dance) for the duration of the discussion watching, listening and making notes without intervention. The more the group drifts from what the bad listener perceives to be the point, the better. The bad listener still has to sit there listening to it all without being allowed to offer any clarifications or corrections.

- After twenty minutes or so invite the bad listener to paraphrase the ideas he/she has noted without demure while the group members check that all their ideas were heard.

Bad listeners suffer agonies while playing wallflower because they are committed to the topic under discussion and yet are condemned to the role of silent note-taker.

However you choose to go about it, providing your people with opportunities to develop their listening skills is an invaluable contribution to all their learning and development. Tempting though it is, it is never safe to take listening for granted.

58 Market testing

Market testing is usually seen as a threatening activity that no-one in their right mind would subject themselves to. People who have market testing imposed on them invariably regard it as a vote of no confidence. The message seems to be 'there is someone out there who would do your job better and be more cost effective'. But the process of tendering for your own job in direct competition with outside suppliers provides an excellent antidote to complacency and, a profound learning experience.

Market testing done properly tests the efficiency of an in-house service by exposing it to competition from outside contractors. The in-house team currently doing the work are therefore required to bid in direct competition with others. The whole exercise is carried out on a 'level playing field' with the in-house team being treated exactly like an ordinary contractor. The overall aim is to secure value for money.

Market testing thus makes people look hard for improvements in efficiency and cost their activities. It is inevitable that this supreme test, with such high stakes, forces people to learn hard lessons. Admittedly the lessons spring from adversity but some of the most profound learning is generated by difficulties, problems and mistakes.

You can create your own mini-version of the market testing experience by imposing an exercise where each of your people has to justify their existence. It is best if the element of competition is retained, either by inviting an appropriate outside agency to put in a tender for the work, or by getting another insider to do so.

Even if it is not feasible to have competitive tenders, real or contrived, it is still worth getting each of your subordinates to make a case for the continuance of his/her job. A version of the 'balloon debate' would provide a suitable formula for this where it is imagined that each job is in a basket beneath a crippled hot air balloon which is rapidly losing height. A certain number of jobs have to be sacrificed, ie be jettisoned from the balloon, in order to save others. Each job holder has to argue the worthwhileness and added value of their contribution in direct competition with the arguments marshalled by others. A vote is then taken to see which jobs 'survive' and which get the push.

Competing with others, whether in a fully fledged market test or in the equivalent of a balloon debate, concentrates the mind wonderfully. The process of justifying their existence gets people not only to evaluate their contribution but also to argue it convincingly. Win or lose, learning is the inevitable consequence.

59 Marketing

Marketing is so basic that it isn't sensible to consider it a different function or leave it to the experts. Everyone has customers and, since marketing is seeing the business from the customer's point of view, *everyone* is a marketeer. Marketing involves finding out who your customers are, and what they need, and designing products or services that exceed their expectations. In essence, marketing is an outside-in, rather than an inside-out approach; it means looking at your offerings not to see what you put in, but to see what your customers get out.

There are a number of things you can do to get your people to operate as marketeers. You could get them to do an exercise to establish their customers' needs involving interviews or a survey or both (see 24, Conducting surveys and 51, Interviewing). You could get them to anticipate their customers' needs by analysing current needs and indulging in a little forecasting (see 41, Forecasting). You could get them to segment their customers, ie identify groups of customers who behave in a similar way, and plan different strategies to satisfy different segments. Finally, you could get your people to describe their products and services in terms of their customer benefits, as distinct from the features and supposed advantages of the products themselves.

If this all seems a little daunting, there are some warm up exercises you could do to get people into the swing of things. For example, ask people to assume that they themselves are 'a product' and to identify their distinctive competence and the benefits of these for their 'customers', ie anyone they have dealings with. This 'if you were a product' exercise often triggers some useful realizations about the worthwhileness for customers of a product; in particular that the 'worth of a thing is what it will bring'. *Anything*, people skills, specific products or services, lends itself to a bit of marketing.

Lessons learned from marketing activities are likely to include

- everyone has customers

- it's not good enough to do good things; you have to let people know you are doing them

- the purpose of any business is to create customers

- until customers have information about what is available they have no real freedom of choice

- marketing is all about leading customers where they want to go before they know it themselves

- it isn't enough to meet customers' needs; they have to be exceeded

- since you can't please everyone all the time, you need to narrow the focus and give superior customer service to 'segmented' customers ie don't try to be all things to all customers.

Conclusions such as these, and others that flow from the processes involved in adopting a marketing approach, have the potential to make a vast difference to customer service. You might even urge your subordinates to treat you as one of their customers (but only, perhaps, if you are prepared to regard them as an important segment of *your* customers).

60 Meetings

Meetings have a reputation for being boring but that is only because they aren't used as opportunities to develop people. Any meeting, big or small, routine or controversial, planned or unplanned, long or short, is literally packed with interesting things from which to learn.

Broadly, lessons learned are likely to fall into three categories

- what is learned from the subject matter discussed at the meeting

- what is learned from the way the meeting was *structured,* ie the objectives, agenda and time-keeping aspects

- what is learned from the way the participants *behaved* during the meeting.

Oddly enough, the first category, the subject matter, is the least fruitful from a learning point of view. Of course, the whole idea of having a meeting is to decide something, plan something, agree something, gather people's views about something, or to inform people about something. There would be no point in having a meeting unless there was at least one 'something', ie a topic that was worth bringing people together for. It is likely, therefore, that everyone at the meeting will increase their knowledge and understanding of the topic or subject matter.

Fine. But the subject matter is but a fraction of what can be learned at any meeting if it is used as a learning opportunity. Consider the following possibilities to do with the *structure* and organization of meetings

- how to set objectives for meetings which describe desired outcomes that are measurable

- the best process to use to get the objectives agreed and understood by all the participants

- the advantages of circulating an agenda before the

meeting or whether it is best to agree an agenda at the start (or not to have an agenda at all)

- whether to start with 'information' agenda items and work up to the more demanding collective decision-making items and *vice versa*

- how to get meetings to start and, even more important, finish on time

- the optimum maximum length for a meeting so that it is productive and effective

- the advantages of focused single topic, as opposed to wide-ranging multi-topic, meetings

- the effect of the venue and physical surroundings on meetings (temperature, light, noise, the shape of the table).

Here are more potential lessons to do with the way people *behave* during meetings

- the effect of different participation rates on the meeting, ie contrasts between people who talk often and at length and people who are quiet

- the style of the chairperson and when to be directive and when to be non-directive

- the quality of ideas generated by the meeting and how they are 'processed'

- the ratio of questions to statements

- how often people interrupt and how some people are interrupted whereas other people are not

- the ratio of supports and builds to disagreements and criticisms

- how often there is a summary and the effect summaries have on people's behaviour

- how decisions are reached and whether they are by consensus, majority or acquiescing.

There are a number of ways to boost learning from meetings. Firstly, you can rotate the chair so that different people get the opportunity to have a go and learn from the experience. Secondly, you can have a process review at the end of the normal agenda and share perceptions of what went well and what could have gone better. Thirdly, you can experiment with different aspects of the meeting by, for example, tackling things in an unusual order, changing the venue, making it a standing-room-only meeting, having visitors. Fourthly, you can get someone to be a dispassionate observer at the meeting and give them the right to intervene whenever they want to make a process observation (but ban them from making observations on the topic or task).

None of these ideas is mutually exclusive, so you could do all of them. Meetings need never be boring again.

61 Mentoring

A mentor is an uninvolved confidant and advisor. Confidentiality is of the essence and sessions with a mentor are strictly 'off the record'. It is impossible therefore, for you to mentor your own subordinates. You can, and should, coach them (see 21, Coaching) but always as an *involved* coach. Someone else has to act as their *uninvolved* coach/mentor and respect their confidences.

The best mentors are more experienced than their mentees and have the time and enthusiasm to be an extra source of support, guidance and encouragement. Mentors provide

- an extra perspective

- an extra push when the going gets tough

- an outside, uninvolved objectivity

- an extra role model

- a sounding board and/or shoulder to cry on.

Since you cannot mentor your own people you must either encourage them to fix themselves up with a mentor or, better still, set up a reciprocal arrangement with some of your fellow managers whereby you mentor their subordinates and they mentor yours. The more this can be set up as a formal arrangement with clear commitments and expectations the better. For example, you need to agree how often the mentor and mentee should meet, or talk on the phone, who should initiate the contact, the type of issues the mentor is prepared to help with, whether it is an 'emergency' or 'by appointment only' service. Ground rules for confidentiality should also be spelled out so that the mentees feel safe and can learn to trust their mentor. Clear guidelines on confidentiality also help to avoid embarrassing misunderstandings between you and your subordinate's mentors. Mentors need protection by the equivalent of a hippocratic oath.

The biggest obstacles to successful mentoring are the predictable ones of lack of time, skill and will. It isn't a complete answer, but the more you can incite your subordinates to place demands on their mentors the more likely it is that help will be forthcoming. There is no substitute for a purposeful mentee who is determined to get his/her money's worth out of a mentor. So, when you coach remember to say 'ask your mentor, that's what they're for'.

Your subordinates stand to gain considerable added value from the *combined* help provided by you as their coach and someone else as their mentor. To have one sort of help is obligatory; to have both is ideal.

62 Mission statements

Mission statements are much in vogue at present and most self-respecting organizations have one with a framed copy on the wall in reception for customers to read. The best mission statements clearly define what business the organization is in and spell out a purpose in a clear, unequivocal way. Some examples are

Pepsi:	Beat Coke
Walt Disney:	To make people have fun
Law Society:	To be the best professional organization in the world
Honda Motorcycles:	We will crush, squash and slaughter Yamaha
BT:	To provide world class telecommunications and information products and services
Johnson & Johnson:	We believe our first responsibility is to the doctors, nurses and patients, to mothers and all others who use our products and services
BUPA:	To deliver the best value independent health finance and insurance

Unfortunately most mission statements fail to engender a feeling of purposeful *esprit de corps.* One problem is that organizational mission statements get handed down from on high, the next best thing to tablets of stone, and there is no buy-in. The *fait accompli* is greeted, with a massive 'not invented here' reaction. Another problem is that the mission statement rapidly becomes seriously undermined by conspicuous failures to 'walk the talk'. Discrepancies between the laudable words in the statement and managerial actions serve only to increase cynicism and suspicion.

Despite these problems, the *process* of fashioning and agreeing a succinct statement of purpose is a profound learning experience. It involves much soul-searching as people bring together different perceptions and values (see 20, Clarifying values). The answer, therefore, regardless of whether or not your organization has a mission statement, is to involve your subordinates in an exercise where

- each individual writes down, in a sentence or two, his/her own mission statement

- each individual has a chance to explain his/her mission statement to immediate colleagues with whom they work

- each group or team of colleagues agrees their own communal mission statement.

If you wish, you could then, together with your direct reports, (never alone) agree a departmental mission statement, but, from a learning point of view, this is less important than the 'bottom up' approach involving each individual.

Resist the temptation to mount and frame the statements. It would be more appropriate to ask people what they learned from the process of agreeing a purpose and then throw away all the statements. A couple of months later check to see how many people can remember the essence of their mission statement. If they can't, repeat the whole exercise until your subordinates have learned the value of having a clear purpose to guide their day-to-day actions.

63 Modifying behaviour

Whenever your subordinates complain about someone else's behaviour it is an opportunity to help them work out what to do to improve the situation. Grumbles about what people have done or not done are prevalent in most organizations. Less common is a systematic approach for solving the problems. Instead of merely commiserating, or telling people not to whinge, you can help people solve their own problems and give them a learning experience all at the same time.

Behavioural problems fall into two categories, either they are uncharacteristic one-offs or they are behaviour patterns that tend to occur again and again and perhaps persist over long periods. The one-off problems are easier to live with and deal with. Giving the offender feedback, for example, is often sufficient to jolt him/her into an apology and, hopefully, corrective action. It is the persistent problems that are the real challenge (and the ones more likely to exasperate your subordinates) and here is a simple step by step routine you can use to help them work out a solution.

Step 1   Ask for a clear description of the behaviour that is considered to be a problem. Insist on a succinct, specific, *observable* behaviour, eg 'He points out snags and difficulties and explains why my idea won't work'.

Step 2   Explore the circumstances that trigger the problem behaviour by asking 'when does he behave like this?' (The question is 'when' *not* 'why'. 'Why' invites retrospective speculation about the origins of the behaviour, whereas 'when' sticks to the here and now and the connection between events and the behaviour in question.) Possible triggers might be

-    when an idea for change is presented as a *fait accompli*

-    when there has been no consultation

-    when the idea is first broached in a meeting with colleagues present

-     when so and so is the idea-haver.

Step 3   Explore what happens after the behaviour has occurred by asking 'what does he gain from behaving like this?' Possible pay-offs might be

-     the idea gets dropped or modified

-     the idea-haver has a rough time, ie he is 'punished' for not consulting

-     the objector gets lots of attention

-     the objector is covered and can always say 'I told you so'.

Step 4   Get a clear description of the desired behaviour (usually the opposite of the problem behaviour).

Step 5   Invite your subordinate to work out how he/she could change the circumstances that trigger the problem behaviour (Step 2) and, instead, trigger the desired behaviour, eg by indulging in some one-to-one consulting, avoiding *fait accomplis* and having the idea presented more skilfully.

Step 6   Invite your subordinate to work out how to arrange things so that there are greater gains for the person in being positive than negative, eg the idea gets improved, the person still gets lots of attention, more when positive, less when negative.

The first three steps focus on the 'befores and afters' of the current situation and how they trigger and reinforce the problem behaviour. The second three steps concentrate on how to change the situation in order to modify the behaviour.

Your subordinates stand to learn much by being helped through these steps. For example, they will discover that

-     behaviour never happens in a void; it always has its roots in the surrounding situation or circumstances

-   it is more practical to concentrate on modifying outward, manifest behaviour than to attempt to change underlying attitudes and emotions

-   it is always possible to understand why people persist with certain behaviour patterns; their experience has shown it works often enough to bring them gains

-   nagging people to change their behaviour is futile unless it is supported by appropriate changes to the situation

-   most persistent behavioural problems are unwittingly created and reinforced by a system of rewards and punishments that make up the 'culture' of the organization.

If, whenever they have a people-problem, you can help your subordinates to work through the six steps, you will have done them a considerable service.

They might see how to anticipate and prevent behavioural problems instead of just fixing them. They might even start to modify your behaviour so that you do more to help them learn and develop.

64 Negotiating

Negotiating is an activity that seeks to reach agreement between two or more different starting positions. Everyone has to negotiate from time to time in order to secure enough of what they want - especially when resources are limited. Negotiating is a fascinating process festooned with lessons to learn that transfer to many other types of interaction.

Negotiations have six possible outcomes:

> **Win - lose**
> 'I'll get my way; you won't get yours'
>
> **Lose - win**
> 'You'll probably get your way; I won't get mine'
>
> **Lose - lose**
> 'If I can't get my way, I'll make sure you can't get yours'
>
> **Win**
> 'I'll secure my way and leave you to see if you can secure yours'
>
> **Win - win**
> 'It's not my way or your way - let's look for a better way'
>
> **No - deal**
> 'If we can't find a way that benefits us both; let's agree to disagree'

From a learning standpoint win-win negotiations are the best to practise. This is not to imply that the other five possible outcomes are 'wrong' (there are appropriate times for each) merely that the skills required to accomplish a win-win outcome are more considerable and therefore stretch people more.

You can easily provide your subordinates with opportunities to indulge in win-win negotiations. The negotiations do not have to be with suppliers or customers or union representatives, you can create 'small n' negotiations in a variety of ways. For example, whenever your subordinates want something from you, be it your time, your help, your agreement or a decision, you can negotiate with them. Whenever your subordinates ask you to settle a conflict about resources or a difference of opinion about the best way forward, you can challenge them to negotiate a win-win resolution.

Here are some of the gems your subordinates will learn from negotiating

- the need for thorough homework and knowing the relevant facts, figures and arguments

- the need to start by agreeing a procedure, particularly a purpose, and the importance of starting with some agreements to establish a win-win climate

- the need to exchange brief opening statements spelling out the two starting positions and desired outcomes

- the importance of questions of clarification (not justification), listening and summarising

- how to use 'and' thinking, as opposed to 'either or' thinking

- how to focus on the reasons behind the positions people take up, rather than attacking the positions or the people

- how to explore the pros and cons of all ideas rather than counter proposing, which is always perceived as disagreeing rather than being constructive

- how to avoid 'irritators', especially exaggerations, and instead stick to the facts and keep the emotional temperature down

- how to disagree constructively by reversing the way people usually disagree, ie not saying 'I disagree because...', but giving the reasons *before* saying 'I disagree'.

There are numerous other lessons, to do with both tactics and
behaviour, to learn from negotiating. Since so many things at
work have to be negotiated you might as well encourage the use
of win-win behaviours amongst your subordinates. That way, you
stand to gain as much as they do.

65 Networking

Whenever people get together with a common interest and swop experiences they are networking. Sharing information with people you would not normally meet is a potent learning brew but it has to be triggered by an 'event' or else it tends to be one of those ideas that is nice in theory but gets squeezed out in practice.

Your only task is to bring people together. Once that has been accomplished, networking will be the inevitable consequence.

There are a number of ways you could trigger networking ranging from informal to formal. Perhaps the most informal is to ensure that your people have a place to congregate and an excuse to do so. Over a coffee break or lunch break might suffice. If you want to broaden the membership of the network you could invite people from different functions, but with a common interest, to meet and compare notes. Alternatively, you could be more formal and organize a conference, with a few speakers to stimulate debate, but with plenty of time for participants to mingle, converse and learn from each other (see 28, Creating your own workshop).

If you want your people to network with people outside your organization, then encourage them to join external interest groups or professional bodies and/or to attend one day seminars where people with similar interests are likely to gather through a process of self-selection.

Besides acquiring useful information specific to a given topic or issue, your people stand to learn a number of valuable things from networking. For example they will discover that

- people everywhere share similar concerns and problems

- swopping experiences is a more powerful way to learn than listening to the 'experts' or gurus

- asking and answering questions and active listening are the only three behaviours you need to network effectively

- the claim that 'it isn't what you know but who you know that counts' is cynical and untrue. The truth is 'it's what you know *from* who you know that counts'.

Whilst 'old boy' networks have an understandable reputation for being elitist, no-one doubts their power to influence. 'Learning' networks by contrast, provide all participants with equal opportunities to learn and develop and are above suspicion. Stimulate networking and you'll stimulate learning.

66 Offering encouragement

The simple act of offering encouragement gives a powerful boost to people's endeavours to learn and develop. Learning has its ups and downs and a brief word of encouragement can help to enthuse someone who is flagging or perhaps on the verge of giving up. Bleak stages in learning are when someone

- has had a perplexing experience and can't yet 'see the wood for the trees'

- has a long held paradigm that has been threatened or challenged

- feels 'out of their depth', stupid, inept or embarrassed

- feels that long term gains will not adequately compensate for short term losses and that it isn't worth the effort to persevere.

It is at times like these, when people feel vulnerable and are inclined to retreat into their comfort zones, that you need to rejuvenate them with some timely encouragement.

All the best learning and development involves going at risk and experimenting (see 38, Experimenting) and many people have learned from bitter experience to be cautious and play safe. This is why your encouragement and support has such an important part to play.

You can encourage your people in two rather different ways. First, by being a role model and being seen to be a continuous learner/developer yourself. You can be sure your subordinates are watching you and quickly detect discrepancies between 'do as I say' and 'do as I do'. You can become a walking, talking, living advertisement for continuous development by

- doing explicit reviews of your own successes, mistakes and experiences and drawing lessons from them (see 78, Reviewing learning)

145

- soliciting feedback from your subordinates and acting upon it (see 95, Upward appraisal/feedback)

- being an experimenter yourself by trying out better/different ways of doing things (see 38, Experimenting)

- talking openly about what you are learning/have learned.

All these are ways of manifestly demonstrating that you are doing it yourself and this will encourage the faint hearted.

The second way you can encourage people is simply to urge *them* to have a go. Clearly this has more credibility if you are having a go yourself but even so it is always worth frequently offering words of encouragement. If you do this you will pre-empt the oft quoted 'it is easier to ask for forgiveness than for permission'. Encouraging people *is* giving them permission and it is astonishing how many people seem to need it before they are prepared to 'go for it'.

67 Organizing an event

All the best events, unless they are completely spontaneous, need organizing. The organizer stands to learn much from all that is involved in masterminding the occasion. Each time you delegate the organizing of an event, in effect you give someone a mini-project to undertake (see 74, Project work) with a start, middle and end. In the normal course of events there are lots of opportunities to delegate a bit of organizing. For example, you could give different subordinates at different times the task of organizing

- a meeting

- an outside visit to a customer, supplier, government body, educational institution, etc.

- a customer hospitality event

- a demonstration or exhibition

- an office party

- an open day

- a fund-raising event

- a sports meeting

- a course or conference

- an induction programme

- an itinerary for an overseas business trip

- a leaving or long service presentation

- a prize-giving event.

All these events, and others like them, are well worth delegating, not only to get the show on the road but because they provide such useful learning opportunities. The advantage of a mini-project that lasts only days, or at most a few weeks, is that the whole cycle of planning, doing and reviewing is completed quickly enough for the whole experience to be fresh in people's minds. Contrasting what was planned with what actually happened is often a salutary experience with lessons to learn about the perils of over-planning and under-planning.

If you feel brave enough, delegate the organizing of an event to a subordinate who would not normally undertake those duties. To do so gives him/her an extra challenge and a 'buzz' from the opportunity itself and the recognition it brings. If this seems foolhardy, you can step up the number of interim reviews and turn each into a coaching session (see 21, Coaching).

68 Persuading and influencing

In a sense, all conversations between people at work involve influencing. Just think how many times your subordinates 'lobby' you in an attempt to influence a decision, get you to change your mind about something or persuade you to do something. Explicitly or implicitly the aim of most communication between people is to influence. Whenever, therefore, your subordinates attempt to persuade you, it automatically provides a learning opportunity - if only you can get them to see it that way.

There are a number of influencing techniques you can help your subordinates to develop which will stand them in good stead as persuaders. Watch for the following, did he/she

- ask you questions to establish your starting position?

- set a realistic objective in the light of your starting position?

- capture your interest with an initial benefit statement, ie say how you stood to gain?

- go on to describe other potential benefits?

- offer 'evidence' to back up the benefits being claimed?

- attempt to defuse some of your objections *before* you raised them?

- finish with a summary of the idea and its main benefits?

- sound enthusiastic?

- look at you for about half the time and make plenty of eye contact?

Any or all of these aspects are excellent lessons for your subordinates and it is more powerful to use real pieces of persuasion that crop up in the normal working day than artificially contrived role-playing exercises that are typically used on courses. Whenever your subordinates seek to influence you, which is often, you have an opportunity to coach (see 21, Coaching) handed to you on a plate.

69 Planning

Planning, whether it be a long term strategic plan or a short term plan for a one-off event, is a process from which there is much to learn. Planning concentrates the mind in a way nothing else can. It combines looking forward, with all its inevitable uncertainties, and attention to detail; an odd, almost paradoxical, mixture.

Of course, the whole idea of a plan is to have something that can be implemented, but since the acts of planning and implementing are quite separate and distinct, it is possible to generate planning opportunities without applying the ultimate test of implementation. Perhaps this is why Eisenhower said 'plans are nothing. Planning is everything'. If you think of planning as a developmental opportunity, rather than as something that must be implemented, it will open up numerous extra possibilities. You could get your subordinates to plan

- a specific event (see 67, Organizing an event)

- a project (see 74, Project work)

- a product or service launch

- the annual budget for your department

- a five year strategic plan for your department

- a business plan for the whole organization.

The last idea in the above list may strike you as unduly ambitious but it calls for some in-depth analysis of the organization's past and current performance and gives people an appreciation of the 'big picture'. It has been used successfully as an induction project for graduates entering the world of industry and commerce for the first time.

Whilst there is much to learn from planning as such, undoubtedly the best plans from a learning and development point of view are ones that the planners will have to implement. A comparison between what was planned and what actually happened is often a salutary experience, with many deviations from the plan either because of inadequacies in the plan itself or because of unexpected events that hadn't been anticipated and for which there were no contingencies.

Perhaps the most useful planning/implementing activity you can get your subordinates to undertake is to plan their own development. This has the double attraction of helping them to take responsibility for their own development and, at the same time, generate practice in planning skills. Personal development plans can focus on the acquisition of knowledge or skills or techniques - in fact *anything* that meets an identified need and will contribute to improved performance. The best development plans are

- feasible; all things considered it should be possible to implement the plan

- immediate; focus on aspects it is possible and useful to develop *now* rather than things that might or might not have longer term usefulness

- selective; tackle development needs one by one rather than taking on too much concurrently

- specific; spell out precise actions, with i's dotted and t's crossed, and deadlines.

Encouraging your subordinates to produce personal development plans means 'contracting' to do your bit to help both in the devising and implementation of the plans and in reviewing their success or otherwise (see 78, Reviewing learning and 55, Learning contracts).

One of the most telling lessons from any planning activity is the discovery that things rarely go according to plan ('the best laid plans of mice and men...') and that the main purpose of planning is *to have something to change.* The fact that plans need constant adaption as events unfold does not prove the futility of planning. The real indictment is slavishly sticking to a plan that is screaming out to be modified.

Planning generates lessons galore!

70 Praising

Whenever you praise something that someone has done you reinforce the behaviour, ie make it more likely he/she will repeat it again, and provide positive feedback (see 43, Giving feedback) from which the person can learn.

In this punitive world criticisms tend to outnumber praise (see 30, Criticizing). But we need a mixture of both. Since there is no perception without contrast, praise would be diminished without criticism and *vice versa*. Praise tends to have a motivating effect on people's performance as well as doubling up as feedback from which to learn.

To praise in a way that enhances learning and development, adopt the following guidelines

- always give specific praise and avoid meaningless generalizations. Start with what you have observed, or heard from someone else, then go on to spell out why you liked it

- always praise better-than-expected results or actions. For example, when people exceed their target, make an extra effort, are punctual when usually late, and so on

- always use 'stand alone' praise and do not dilute it with any criticism. The rule is when praise is deserved, give it; when criticism is deserved, give it. Don't mix the two

- always praise as close in time to the person's action as possible. Praising someone a long time after the event is still worthwhile but has less impact

- always praise authentically, not because you think you should or only on special occasions or to impress a third party.

Praise is one of the most effective and yet inexpensive ways to motivate people. When you also realize that it helps people to learn it's a wonder it isn't more prevalent. From praise people are likely to learn

- that their efforts are recognized

- that the world isn't such a negative/punitive place after all

- which actions/behaviours meet with approval and therefore need to happen more often

- which actions/behaviours don't attract praise and therefore need revision

- that if praise gives them such a warm glow, then perhaps they in turn should praise others more often

- how to accept praise graciously without self-deprecation and embarrassment.

Remember that feedback, whether it be praise or criticism, is the essence of learning and development and that most of us would rather be ruined by praise, than helped with criticism.

71 Presenting

Making effective presentations is an essential skill, certainly as people climb the managerial ladder, and every presentation generates masses of learning opportunities. Many people find the prospect of making presentations daunting, if not traumatic. The answer is to give them a push and initially provide relatively 'safe', low risk opportunities to present and gradually step up the odds. Presenting is a clear case of 'if you do the thing you fear, the fear will disappear'.

You can easily make opportunities for your people to present. Start with talks to outside organizations (see 45, Giving outside talks) where, should things go wrong, the people in the audience need never be seen again. Then progress to 'parochial' presentations within the compass of bigger departmental meetings. Always give the presenter feedback (see 43, Giving feedback) after a presentation. Gradually increase the challenge by inviting your people to present to larger audiences, to more senior people and to people who really matter, like customers. Likely lessons learned from giving presentations include

- the importance of knowing your audience, who they are, their level of knowledge, what they need to know

- the need to plan the talk carefully and to leave nothing to chance

- the importance of structuring the talk in three segments; the beginning, the middle and the end

- the need to rehearse and not be over-dependent on written notes

- the usefulness of visual aids, however primitive

- the importance of personal anecdotes and jokes to enliven the talk and capture and retain the audience's interest

- the importance of spreading eye contact around and not looking at a fixed person or spot

- the importance of movement and gestures to emphasize a point but not to distract or irritate the audience.

- how to *sound* enthusiastic and in control even when you are not

- how to judge what amount of material will fit into a given amount of time

- how to handle questions from the audience.

There is no doubt that presenting is an invaluable aid to learning and development. The sooner you can start your people on the presenting trail, the more confident they will become. Even if they don't thank you at the time, they'll be grateful when they look back - especially when they become accomplished after-dinner speakers!

72 Process re-engineering

Process re-engineering is a 'fresh-start' approach aimed at radical change. It comes from the 'if it ain't broke, break it' school of thought and by no stretch of the imagination could be considered to be tinkering or cosmetic. Strictly speaking, process re-engineering is a top down, 'holistic' approach to change that transcends departmental and functional boundaries. Now this is a heresy, but you can take a leaf out of the process re-engineering book and do your own within the confines of your own department. Clearly this will be but a pale shadow of the real thing but none-the-less a fundamental look at your own processes will generate some powerful lessons for all concerned.

In process re-engineering speak you manage a series of processes. A process is defined as 'any activity or group of activities that takes an input, adds value to it, and provides an output to an internal or external customer' (from Business Process Improvement by H Harrington published by McGraw-Hill). Everything is therefore a process from the acceptance of an order, to the design and manufacture of goods and services to invoicing and the collection of money. Your department may only contribute in a small way to the total process, but the fact that you have jurisdiction over some processes (and you do) means you can indulge in some re-engineering.

These are the steps you and your subordinates need to go through.

1. Find out what your customers really want. Use questionnaires, surveys, customer focus groups, *anything* that helps you see your business from the customers' point of view.

2. Instead of saying 'the system won't allow it' or 'I wouldn't start from here', imagine you have a clean slate and no constraints and ask yourself

   - in the light of what my customers really want, what is the vision for the future?

   - what performance criteria must we aspire to to achieve the vision?

157

- what processes will we need to achieve the criteria?

3. Map out and measure the existing processes. Draw flow-charts and understand them in detail. Where do they fail to give your customers what they really want ?

4. Resist the temptation merely to tinker with the existing processes (you can always fall back on this if the re-engineered solution is too radical). Instead be brave and start again, mapping out processes that will give your customers what they really want.

5. Implement the new processes or, if you are faint hearted, modifications to the old ones.

Many of the lessons to be learned from process re-engineering come from the 'intellectual' process of going through steps one to four above. It is the continual re-appraisal of customer wants and existing systems that provides the perfect antidote to complacency. Your subordinates will discover that

- nothing is sacrosanct, everything is challengeable

- when things go wrong it is invariably due to inadequacies in the processes, not the people

- change really is permanent

- there is no gain without pain.

Process re-engineering is change writ large and wherever there is change there is learning and development. Getting your subordinates critically to appraise processes that have been taken for granted, or outlived their usefulness, will result in delighted customers and developing subordinates.

73 Producing one-pagers

Summarizing, whether orally or in writing, is a useful skill as well as providing a learning opportunity for the summarizer. In order to summarize something accurately you need to understand it at a deeper level than passive listening or reading normally provides. The intense search for the essentials is the key to this deeper understanding and the discipline of getting all the salient points on to one side of A4 calls for greater ruthlessness than would otherwise be the case.

There are numerous opportunities to invite your subordinates to produce one-pagers. The following spring to mind immediately

-	papers that are issued as essential reading prior to attending meetings

-	written reports both internal and external

-	articles in newspapers, trade journals and management magazines

-	handouts from courses, conferences and seminars

-	books (try this one).

Getting your subordinates to produce one-pagers for you is a classic win-win. You win by having a nice succinct summary of something you need to know about, and they win by being better informed and acquiring an invaluable skill which will stand them in good stead throughout their careers.

Enough said (it would be hypocritical to produce more than one page on this subject).

74 Project work

Almost any plan, scheme or task can be thought of as a project. There are big formal projects that may rumble on for years, for example in the construction industry or in research and development. There are small, less formal projects that may be completed in just weeks or months, for example an office relocation or the introduction of new technology or an investigation into how to improve some aspect of the business. All projects, big or small, are discrete, temporary assignments ultimately aimed at increasing revenue or reducing costs.

Projects are usually undertaken by a team, or a task force, specially convened for the life of the project. For large, lengthy projects, people might be seconded as full time members of the team, whereas smaller projects are often tackled on a part-time basis with the project work bolted on as an 'extra' to normal, everyday duties. Whichever way it is done, the joy of project work from a learning and development viewpoint is that it creates for the people involved a special experience for a finite length of time, that transcends their usual day to day activities. It is the relative novelty of project work plus the fact that projects are perceived as being important with high visibility (otherwise they wouldn't have been set up as projects in the first place) that makes them an attractive, even heady, mixture for those involved.

You can turn any task of substance into a project by spelling out clear terms of reference for the project, including objectives, constraints and a completion date. All projects should have a sponsor, or a client, a project manager, or leader, and a team of people who bring together different perspectives, thus making it possible for them to thrive on the differences and achieve synergy. Possible tasks suitable for project work are many and various including

- how to identify business opportunities

- how to exploit a new business opportunity once it has been identified

- how to reduce costs without having an adverse effect on revenues/profits

- how to handle and resolve customer complaints

- how to improve productivity

- how to launch and market a new product/service

- how to make meetings less time-consuming and more effective

- how to improve safety

- how to reduce absenteeism

- how to communicate essential information quickly and accurately

- how to use competencies to improve the selection, appraisal and promotion of staff.

The possibilities are endless. The most challenging projects, and therefore the best from a developmental point of view, are ones where the project team has responsibility not just for producing recommendations but also for implementation. If you also write learning into the terms of reference, ie 'progress reports must always include a description of lessons learned from the experience of the project', you have an intriguing recipe for much learning and development.

The sort of lessons learned depend on the size and length of the project and whether it requires participants to do the assignment on top of, or instead of, their normal work. Typical generic lessons (each will spawn numerous specifics) from project work include

- coping with ambiguous situations

- relying on the expertise and knowledge of other people, ie learning that you can't be an expert in everything

- getting co-operation from a diverse mixture of people, with different perspectives, over whom you have no authority

- the effect of a finite time frame on getting things done

- making sense of contradictory, 'messy' data

- persevering through adversity

- recognising and seizing opportunities.

In addition, other lessons, for example about teamwork (see 92, Teamwork) and, of course, from the subject matter of the project itself will be learned.

It is worth noting that when people reminisce about formative experiences in their careers, project work gets practically more mentions than anything else. Give your subordinates projects to tackle and you could get a mention in their memoirs!

75 Reading

'You learn to read and you read to learn' goes one clever play on words and there is no doubt that if you get your people to read relevant material, they will acquire useful knowledge. Reading, in common with all other acquired skills, improves with practise. People read faster and with better comprehension if they read passages of prose on a daily basis.

You can help people 'read to learn' by feeding them with things to read. Active reading, ie when someone has to make notes on, summarize or communicate the essence of what they have read, is better than passive reading. Most managers complain that they have too much to read, so why not selectively delegate some of your reading thus having less to read yourself and providing your delegatees with learning opportunities they wouldn't otherwise have? For example, you could delegate

- scanning daily newspapers for relevant articles and news items (thus creating your own cuttings agency)

- reading and summarizing articles from trade and/or management journals

- reading and summarizing internal reports and the pile of papers often issued before management meetings.

Additionally, you could regularly allocate specific reading projects to people where, say, a book on management or quality or interpersonal skills or whatever, could be given to someone to read and report back on by an agreed date. The same treatment could be used to ensure your people read the company's annual report and those of your competitors.

Of course, you may have subordinates who already read a great deal as an integral part of their job. In this case, ensure that any extra reading you impose on them is a realistic requirement and preferably give them reading material which, whilst relevant, goes beyond what they would normally read.

For other subordinates, who don't have to read much in the normal course of events, keep dishing out the reading. If at first they find it difficult, don't be put off by their protests. Persevere in the sure knowledge that they will find it easier as they become more practised and that you are providing them with worthwhile learning opportunities. If information is power, this is one way to empower your subordinates.

76 Rehearsing

Many people operate on the optimistic assumption 'that it will be alright on the night' and leave to chance things which would have benefited from a run-through. Rehearsals are learning experiences in their own right. In fact, very often there is more to learn from a rehearsal than from the real thing. This is because in a rehearsal everyone is in experimental, 'suck it and see' mode. The willingness to give it a go and learn from a process of trial and error is higher when rehearsing than it is when the pressure is on to perform well and not make mistakes. Conformity and caution reduce learning opportunities.

Because people tend to skimp on rehearsing, and learning from it, you should insist on a rehearsal and review for all presentations made by your staff. The best way to enforce this is to represent the audience at the rehearsal yourself. Your presence and your feedback will automatically send out messages about the importance of rehearsing. If it is impossible to attend in person, or if your staff are rehearsing a presentation which is eventually destined for you, then to have two or three uninvolved people act as the audience makes the rehearsal seem more worthwhile and purposeful than merely doing it in front of a mirror.

If a rehearsal is not feasible, perhaps because of time pressures, then the next best thing is for you to insist on a thorough briefing. Whilst describing what it is proposed to do is no substitute for a full blown rehearsal, it is a great deal better than nothing. The act of talking aloud is far more punctilious than just thinking it through in your head.

Rehearsals, besides being splendid antidotes to complacency, are likely to generate a number of valuable lessons such as

- the worthwhileness of paying attention to detail

- the need consciously to speak more slowly when you feel nervous

- the need to guard against certain unconscious verbal habits such as saying 'you know', 'actually', 'OK' and non-verbal mannerisms such as wringing hands, finger pointing, foot shuffling

-       how to identify, and plan for, potential weaknesses
        in a presentation where things are more likely to go
        wrong for example, hand over points between
        presenters, unwelcome questions from the audience,
        unspontaneous humour which is supposed to sound
        spontaneous and so on

-       the need to check out, and practise using, visual aid
        equipment and to have contingency plans if it fails.

Perhaps the most overwhelming lesson learned at a rehearsal is
the crucial part feedback has to play. Feedback is more likely to
be sought and given at a rehearsal than at other times where
embarrassment on both sides inhibits. For the essential part
feedback has to play in the whole process of learning and
development see section 43, Giving feedback.

Rehearsals are a way, not to disprove, but to circumvent Murphy's
Law; if anything can go wrong, it will. At least if things are going
to go wrong (and they will) it is better they do so at a rehearsal.

77 Resolving conflicts

Every difference of opinion, every disagreement, is a conflict, either with a big or small c depending on the magnitude of the difference. Conflicts between people are inevitable as they try to agree priorities, make decisions, solve problems and work together. If there weren't differences of opinion it would probably be a sign that people were apathetic or acquiescing by ostensibly saying yes, but in reality hiding major reservations.

Whilst conflicts are rarely welcomed they offer splendid opportunities to

- reach a better solution than would have been possible if the conflict hadn't arisen

- learn from the experience of facing the conflict squarely and addressing it constructively.

It sounds pious to say it, but as a manager the way you handle conflicts is a decisive factor in whether they will result in win-win or win-lose outcomes and whether they will result in beneficial learning.

Broadly there are three different ways to react to conflict

1. Avoid it. Typically this involves

    - denying the conflict exists

    - circumventing the person/people with whom you are in conflict

    - deciding not to make the conflict explicit or to raise it

2. Diffuse it. This involves

    - smoothing things over, 'pouring oil on troubled waters'

    - saying you'll come back to it (as opposed to

dealing with the conflict there and then)

- only dealing with minor points, not the major issues

3. Face it. This involves

    - openly admitting conflict exists

    - explicitly raising the conflict as an issue

All three approaches are genuine options when conflicts arise. There may be occasions when it is best to let it go (why win the battle but lose the war?) and there will be other occasions when some pussy-footing is appropriate. Usually however, facing conflict rather than avoiding it or diffusing it offers the most potential. But *how* you face it makes all the difference. You can face it aggressively or assertively.

People who face conflict *aggressively*

- are secretive about their real objectives
- exaggerate their case
- refuse to concede that the other person has a valid point
- belittle the other person's points
- repeat their case dogmatically
- disagree
- interrupt the other person.

People who face conflict *assertively*

- are open about their objectives
- establish what the other person's objectives are
- search for common ground
- state their case clearly
- understand the other person's case
- produce ideas to solve the differences
- build on and add to the other person's ideas
- summarize to check understanding/agreement.

You can convert conflicts into useful learning opportunities by refusing to adjudicate and doing everything you can to foster assertive behaviour amongst the protagonists. If you put your energies into helping them to find some common ground, however tenuous, and to build on it, then you not only make a constructive resolution more likely, you also make people work for it and learn as they do so.

Lessons learned from resolving conflicts include

- the realization that avoiding and diffusing conflict, whilst tempting, are invariably damage limitation cop-outs

- the discovery that assertiveness breeds assertiveness

- a dawning that there are six possible outcomes to any conflict

  - Win-Lose

    'I'll get my way; you won't get yours.'

  - Lose-Win

    'You'll get your way; I won't get mine.'

  - Lose-Lose

    'If I can't get my way, I'll make sure you can't get yours.'

  - Win

    'I'll secure my way and leave you to secure yours.'

  - Win-Win

    'It's not my way or your way - let's look for a better way.'

- No Deal

    'If we can't find a way that benefits us both, let's agree to disagree.'

- the realization that win-win is the only worthwhile resolution to any conflict, and, failing that, the wisdom of settling for no deal rather than one of the other outcomes

- the realization that when someone takes up an intransigent position it is counter-productive to step up persuasive arguments in an attempt to get the other person to relinquish their position. It is much more productive to establish the reasons behind the position and work out how to accommodate at least some of the reasons in the resolution

- a dawning that conflicts and differences are a sign of people's commitment and passion. By contrast, a lack of conflicts is usually a sign that things are being fudged and/or left to fester.

There is no doubt that each conflict, especially if it is emotionally charged, provides an opportunity to learn and develop *but only if you allow it to.* A yearning to keep things on an even keel, smooth things over and maintain harmony, stunts the learning and lets the protagonists off the hook.

78 Reviewing learning

Whether we recognize it or not, people are learning all the time by putting two and two together, reaching conclusions and modifying their behaviour accordingly. Usually what is learned is unacknowledged and unexplored. It is just left to individuals to learn intuitively by some process of osmosis with no check on what has been learned, its relevance or quality. This is unfortunate for two reasons. Firstly, 'private' learning which isn't promulgated cannot have widespread benefits. It would mean that each individual would have to learn everything first hand instead of learning from other people's shared experiences. Secondly, it is as easy for people to learn the 'wrong' things as it is to learn the 'right' things (see 79, Rewarding the 'right' behaviours) and private learning isn't amenable to scrutiny. Learning reviews overcome these shortcomings by providing opportunities to hold things up to the light and communicate what has been learned.

The most straightforward learning review is where you ask a subordinate what he/she has learned from a recent experience or incident (see 9, Asking questions) and tease out their conclusions and help them to decide what they are going to do better or differently in future. It is easier to surface and make explicit what has been learned if you have got your subordinates to adopt the discipline of keeping learning logs (see 54, Keeping learning logs).

A more ambitious formula for learning reviews is to hold a fortnightly or monthly meeting where a group of your subordinates gather together for a communal review. Each contributor is asked to come to the review with three pieces of information

- a recent experience, good or bad, planned or unplanned, they have had at work

- their conclusions or lessons learned

- their plan to do something better/differently in the light of the conclusions.

The meeting gives an equal amount of air time to each participant and in particular challenges any 'crooked' thinking and tendencies

172

to jump to erroneous or unsubstantiated conclusions. The end result of the review is that each participant has a clear action plan to implement in the interim period before the next learning review.

Learning reviews need not be stand alone occasions. The process of talking about what has been learned is an appropriate 'add on' to many other events that crop up in the normal course of events. A swift, learning review at the end of a meeting is often the key to continually improving the effectiveness of meetings (see 60, Meetings). Learning reviews can be incorporated into coaching sessions (see 21, Coaching).

The whole purpose of reviewing learning is to give people an opportunity to talk about what they have learned. They are learning anyway but too often at a tacit level where the learning is left unarticulated and unshared. Talking about learning makes it explicit and brings added value not least because people can learn so much from each other.

79 Rewarding the 'right' behaviours

By and large people repeat the behaviours that work for them and discontinue the behaviours that don't. Through a rough and ready process of trial and error people gradually build up a repertoire of behaviour patterns. The trouble is that many of these oft repeated behaviours are not especially conducive to learning and development. For example, people have often learned from bitter experience

- to acquiesce and pretend to agree rather than query, question and challenge

- to rubbish ideas rather than suggest them

- to go for expedient quick fixes rather than explain options and weigh up pros and cons

- to be cautious and careful rather than take risks and experiment

- to censor or filter bad news rather than be open about the way it really is

- to blame and justify rather than admit inadequacies and mistakes

- to repeat or cover up mistakes rather than convert them into learning

- to rush around being active rather than reflect, ponder, mull things over and review

- to talk about what has happened, war stories and anecdotes, rather than talk about what has been learned

- to wait for someone else to provide learning opportunities rather than taking responsibility for their own learning and development.

You can do your bit to reverse these tendencies by encouraging the behaviours you want (see 66, Offering encouragement) and, when you get them, leaning over backwards to reward them. The rewards you use need not be lavish, time consuming or expensive. Simple things will do the trick such as

- when your subordinates query, question and challenge, provide full answers, preferably there and then, but if you can't do that, commit to find out and let them know as soon as possible

- when your subordinates suggest ideas, support and build on them

- when your subordinates explore options and weigh up pros and cons, congratulate them and listen to their conclusions

- when your subordinates take risks and experiment, whatever the outcome, praise them for giving it a try (especially if it didn't work out too well)

- when your subordinates are open about the way it is, resist the temptation to 'shoot the messenger' and ask questions to show you are interested in finding out more

- when your subordinates admit inadequacies and mistakes, avoid accusations and blame and instead help to extract lessons learned

- when your subordinates convert their mistakes into learning, acknowledge this and give a recent example of how you have done the same

- when your subordinates reflect, ponder, mull things over and review, show interest and ask for their conclusions/recommendations on future actions

- when your subordinates talk about what they have learned from experience, trade lessons learned by reciprocating with some of your own

-   when your subordinates take responsibility for their own learning and development, ask what you can do to help.

In these small but significant ways you will create a climate where behaviours conducive to learning and development start to flourish and their opposites go into a terminal decline.

It is a gradual process, so be patient. Keep plugging away and you will be rewarded with subordinates who continuously learn and develop and know how to use you as a resource, not as a prop.

80 Rotating jobs

Moving people sideways into a different job, perhaps into a different function, for development purposes is usually easier said than done.   It is often inconvenient to take someone who is accomplished in one job and deliberately put them into another where they have to start near the bottom of the learning curve. It is a good example of a nice idea in theory that has snags in practice.   Of course, purists argue that short term losses in efficiency are more than compensated for in the long run and it is certainly true that learning is accelerated whenever someone is given a new challenge.

If you find it impossible to contemplate rotating your people into different jobs, you might find it more feasible to indulge in some rotation with a small 'r'.   There are numerous tasks that can be rotated, rather than whole jobs, to provide opportunities to learn and develop without going the whole hog. It is just a question of thinking small, breaking jobs up into discrete tasks and working out who would benefit from a go at something different. Here are some examples of tasks you could rotate

- chairing meetings
- acting as minute taker or 'scribe' at meetings
- taking a new starter or visitor on a conducted tour
- answering the telephone
- dealing with customer complaints
- giving a presentation
- analysing some statistical or financial data
- writing a report/drafting letters and memos
- summarising a lengthy book or article into a one-pager
- interviewing customers
- trouble shooting/investigating the cause of a recurring quality problem
- preparing an exhibition
- running a briefing session.

All these small, self contained tasks lend themselves to rotation. You will be able to identify many more depending on the nature of your subordinates' work.

Analogous to rotating tasks is the idea of rotating roles. Within a team, for example, on different occasions different members can undertake different roles. Rotating the co-ordinator's role is perhaps the most obvious, but you could also rotate roles such as challenger, doer, idea-haver, builder, supporter, timekeeper, summarizer and observer. Teams are supposed to thrive on the differences between people, rather than the similarities, and allocating specific roles to different team members helps to ensure the coherence of the team and generates learning opportunities for people as they struggle to master an unfamiliar role.

Job, task and role rotation have long been recognized to have learning and development mileage. It just takes a bit of ingenuity to get it to happen.

81 Sayings and mottos

In offices and on notice boards people often pin up amusing messages such as 'You don't have to be insane to work here, but it helps', and 'The impossible we do at once; miracles take a little longer'. Often these messages, besides having a ring of truth are thought provoking. Examples are 'When all is said and done, far more is said than done' and 'Today is the tomorrow you worried about yesterday'.

The idea, therefore, is to capitalize on similar slogans and messages by having a weekly, fortnightly or monthly slogan about learning and development. For maximum impact, only have one quotation on display at a time and, because familiarity breeds contempt, change the slogan at least each month (more often if you have a plentiful supply of suitable quotations).

To get you started here are some quotations about learning.

> 'It's what you learn after you know it all that counts' (Ethel Barrymore)

> 'Anyone who stops learning is old, whether at twenty or eighty. Anyone who keeps learning stays young. The greatest thing in life is to keep your mind young' (Henry Ford)

> 'You are what you learn'

> 'You are the only person who can take responsibility for your learning and development'

> 'You can't smooth the surf, but you can learn to ride the waves'

> 'There are three versions of an experience
>
> - the one you planned
> - the one you had
> - what you learned from the difference between the two'

'No-one can *make* you learn; only make it more likely that you will'

'Life is just one learning opportunity after another' (after Oscar Wilde)

'Personally I'm always ready to learn, although I do not always like being taught' (Winston Churchill)

'Live and learn!'

'If a little learning is a dangerous thing; you'd better learn a lot' (after Pope)

'Involve me and I understand. Teach me and I forget'

'Development is *always* self-development' (Peter Drucker)

'Complacency is the biggest single enemy of continuous improvement'

'Inside every mistake there are lessons waiting to get out'

'Wise people learn when they can. Fools learn when they must' (after the Duke of Wellington)

'Learning is your only sustainable competitive advantage'

'Learning from experience - the most important of all the life skills'

'Achieving a task is one step forward. Achieving a task and learning from it is two steps forward'

'Become a learning person, not a learned person' (Chris Arygris)

'To a great experience one thing is essential; an experiencing nature' (Walter Bagehot)

'Experience is the greatest teacher - if you learn from it'

'There are two questions to ask yourself each day

- what did I learn yesterday?
- what will I do differently/better today?'

'If it ain't broke; break it - and learn'

'There are three essential conditions for learning; you must be
- able
- willing
- and allowed'

'Change is learning, learning is change; you can't have one without the other'

'Make learning your priority and everything else you achieve will be a welcome spin-off'

'Experience is not what happens to a man; it is what a man does with what happens to him' (Aldous Huxley)

'I would rather entertain people in the hope that they will learn, than teach people in the hope that they will be entertained' (Walt Disney)

'Training is an input. Learning is an output'.

If you changed sayings each month, the above list would last you for two and a half years, by which time you could start the sequence all over again or would have had ample time to collect up some more.

Of course, displaying a slogan doesn't in itself get people to learn and develop; it only acts as a reminder. It is everything else you do that should 'walk the talk'.

82 Searching for opportunities

Opportunities have an uncanny knack of only revealing themselves after the event. With the benefit of hindsight an opportunity becomes apparent but at the time it was missed. This applies both to business and to learning opportunities. It is because opportunities are by their very nature elusive that they need to be consciously and deliberately searched for.

Edward de Bono defines an opportunity as 'a course of action that is possible and obviously worth pursuing'. He claims it is the *possibility* of an opportunity that distinguishes it from wishful thinking. He also argues that there are always more urgent, pressing things to do than look for opportunities and that it is therefore necessary to allocate time for a systematic search. Much of his book 'Opportunities' is given over to proposing a formal system for identifying and auditing business opportunities.

Exactly the same rationale can be applied to learning opportunities; they only exist once they have been seen and they will only be seen if they are looked for. The trick is to stop merely seeing things to do and instead have double vision and see things to do and learn from. In a sense, *everything* that happens, nice or nasty, planned or unplanned, trivial or substantial, is a learning opportunity. The main growth area for learning and development is to couple work-based activities with learning rather than to think of them as separate and distinct activities. The whole of this book is devoted to ideas on how to forge a strong coupling between the two.

You can actively encourage your people to become learning opportunists by instigating regular opportunity searches. Twice a year get each of your subordinates to come up with, say, three ideas for learning opportunities for themselves and three for other people. Each idea must have a description of the potential benefits envisaged both for the person and for the organization. The significant difference between the ideas for 'self' and 'others' is that all the self ones must be opportunities the person has it in their power to do. The ideas for others, on the other hand, ensure you get a steady stream of suggestions and you can decide which, if any, to implement. Hopefully the suggestions that are forthcoming will complement and/or add to many of the ideas in this book.

Ideas which are viable can be built into people's personal development plans or learning contracts (see 55, Learning contracts) or form the basis for a self-development initiative (see 85, Self-development). Needless to say, the peril to guard against is that of dreaming up opportunities that no-one is able or willing to implement.

For additional inspiration read Edward de Bono's book 'Opportunities' published by Pelican Books. All he has to say about business opportunities applies to learning opportunities. Opportunities are there for the taking but only we spot them.

83 Secondments

A secondment is where someone is retained on the payroll but lent to another organization for an agreed period of time, often for a year or more. Some large organizations regularly second senior managers with a wealth of experience to the voluntary sector. To do so is regarded as a mutually advantageous formula. The voluntary organization, strapped for cash, gets a free manager and the donor organization gains a manager who has learned from the novel experience of working in a totally different set up.

From a development point of view, the most potent secondments are where there are stark contrasts between the two working environments; from order to chaos, from centralization to decentralization, from large to small and so on. The greater the contrasts, the more old assumptions, working practices and paradigms are challenged and fresh learning is generated. It is significant that secondments are often cited by those who have experienced them as the time they learned most in their whole career.

You need not contemplate secondment with a big 's' to gain some of the benefits for your staff. It is probably inconceivable to have someone on your headcount who is absent for prolonged periods working elsewhere. Instead, think of secondments with a small 's' where for a day or two, or for a maximum of a week, you lend someone to another department within your organization or, more ambitiously, to an outside body. Obviously short secondments are unlikely to have the full impact of longer ones, but at least they are a realistic second best and still have the potential to generate developmental opportunities that it might not be possible to provide in any other way.

For maximum effect arrange mini-secondments to places where the nature of the work and, preferably, where the whole ethos and culture significantly differ from your own. The whole idea is to use the contrasts as the main stimulus for learning. Always get secondees to articulate what they have learned, irrespective of whether they can see direct and obvious relevance to their normal work.

Predictably, most of the lessons are likely to be about differences rather than similarities; differences in values, in style, in pace, and in quality. Some of the differences will provoke questions about 'why do we do it this way?' and cause a re-examination of things that were previously taken for granted. Some of the lessons will lead to increased confidence that 'we are doing it right' and the realisation that many working practices that had seemed ordinary are in fact superior.

Secondments 'break up the concrete' in rather the same way benchmarking does (see 12, Benchmarking). Both trade on the simple but profound truth that there is no perception without contrast. Give your people contrasts and you will help to open their eyes and heighten their perceptions.

84 Self-assessment questionnaires

People often need a simple way to take stock of their skills and abilities and self-assessment questionnaires are designed to aid and abet such self-examination. The most useful questionnaires for self-assessment purposes

- are short and straightforward to self-administer

- openly explain what the questionnaire is designed to probe

- are simple to self-score

- give advice on how to interpret the score

- suggest ideas for self-development.

Questionnaires are designed to cover a broad spectrum of human attributes from knowledge to aptitudes, from behaviour styles to personality types. Some of the more complex questionnaires have to be administered, scored and interpreted by certified 'experts' under licence but there are plenty that are available for the lay-person and they are the best ones to help with learning and development. The important thing is not to be over-awed by questionnaires and to regard them as a useful way to open up an area that might otherwise be difficult to get at.

One of the hazards with self-assessment is that people's perceptions of themselves may differ significantly from those of other people. This is not necessarily because self-assessees are being deliberately dishonest. It may occur because they genuinely see themselves differently and cannot disentangle their inner motives from their outward actions. When you know your 'heart is in the right place' and your intentions are for the best it can put a different gloss on your behaviour, a gloss that might be lost on other people who can only observe what you say and do. Even when this happens, the questionnaire has served a useful purpose in surfacing differences of perception and making them more amenable to discussion.

The more questionnaire results can be shared and aired the better, but it is even more essential that people commit themselves to some actions to build on strengths and/or overcome weaknesses identified by the questionnaires. These can form the basis of self-development plans or a learning contract (see 85, Self-development and 55, Learning contracts)

When, over thirty years ago, Professor Eysenck published 'Know Your Own IQ' he broke the mould by attacking the cloak of secrecy which had previously shrouded psychometric testing. Since then there has been a gradual increase in openness and in the publication of questionnaires for self-assessment.

Examples of self-assessment questionnaires can be found in the following publications

'The Unblocked Manager' by Mike Woodcock and Dave Francis published by Gower, ISBN 0 566 02373 3

'Test Your Executive Skills' by Terry Farnsworth published by Ebury Press, ISBN 0 85223 635 2

'How Do You Manage?' by John Nicholson published by BBC Books, ISBN 0 563 36335 5

'The Manual of Self-Assessment Questionnaires' written and published by Peter Honey, ISBN 0 9508444 8 9

The latter publication even gives advice on how to devise your own 'home-spun' questionnaires, which is not as difficult or time consuming as you might suppose.

Whether you invent your own or buy them off the shelf, self-assessment questionnaires are a useful way to kick-start learning and development.

85 Self-development

All development is ultimately self-development. The plain fact is that everyone *has* to take responsibility for their own development. In the same way that you can lead a horse to water but you can't force it to drink, you can provide your people with developmental opportunities but they decide whether to take them or not. Of course, it behoves you to make the opportunities enticing and to give active encouragement and support, but that is as much as you can do; the rest is up to them.

Self-development is the development of the self, by the self, through a deliberate process of learning from experience. Through self-development people can

-    increase their knowledge

-    acquire new techniques and skills

-    overhaul their attitudes, beliefs and values

-    become better at managing negative unproductive emotions.

There are only two real constraints on self-development. The first is the individual and how far he/she wishes to go. Some people, for example, are happy to develop their knowledge and skills but hesitate to go deeper into attitudes and emotions.

The second constraint is the climate in the organization which may be fearful of releasing the self-development genie from the bottle. People are only able to take responsibility for their own development if they are allowed to (able, willing *and* allowed).

Some organizations worry that people might become enthusiastic about developing personal attributes which make no obvious contribution to their performance at work. This concern, whilst understandable, fails to recognize the worthwhileness of people acquiring and sustaining the learning habit. The answer, from the organization's point of view, is to help self-developers set learning objectives which benefit *both* the individual and the organization.

You can encourage your people to become self-developers by doing some or all of the following things (all of which are sections in this book).

- Building learning into the system (section 16)
- Funding development (section 42)
- Keeping learning logs (section 54)
- Learning contracts (section 55)
- Offering encouragement (section 66)
- Reviewing learning (section 78)
- Rewarding the 'right' behaviours (section 79)

Best of all, however, is that you become a blatant self-developer yourself. Your people will know you have taken responsibility for your own learning when you

- strive to improve your *current* performance

- deliberately seek out learning opportunities

- extract learning from chance events

- assess your own needs

- set your own development objectives

- assess your own progress

- experiment/try new or different things

- explicitly complete all the stages in the learning cycle (do, review, conclude, plan)

- tolerate short term discomfort in the interests of longer term learning and development.

Just nine explicit indications to your people that you are a self-developer and the way to assess whether they have followed your lead.

86 Setting deadlines

Giving people deadlines is a common, and necessary, activity for any manager. The fascinating business of getting results through other people inevitably means that you need to know completion times for delegated and allocated tasks. (Delegated tasks are ones where you are accountable; allocated tasks are ones where someone else is accountable.)

Attitudes to deadlines vary enormously. In some organizations an agreed deadline is sacrosanct even if heaven and earth have to be moved to meet it. In other organizations deadlines are not taken seriously and there are few adverse consequences for missing them. In macho set-ups imposing impossible deadlines is often a ploy used to sort out the 'men from the boys'. In more enlightened working environments, deadlines are always agreed taking other commitments and priorities into account.

There is much to learn from deadlines, whether agreed or imposed, and each time you set one with a subordinate you are unwittingly providing him/her with a learning opportunity. Examples of lessons learned are

- to speak up assertively and refuse to commit to an unrealistic deadline (you get the deadlines you deserve)

- to give the earliest possible warning and re-negotiate a deadline which, for unforseen reasons, is going to be missed

- how right Northcote Parkinson was when he said 'work expands to fill the time available for its completion'

- the different effects, some motivating some demotivating, of tight deadlines

- how necessity *is* the mother of invention

- how impressive it is to take the initiative and volunteer a self-imposed deadline (even better if you stick to it)

- self-insights into the tendency to procrastinate if a deadline is too lax

- to ask questions and establish the reasons for a deadline

- how to negotiate and reach a win-win deadline that suits all parties

- how to build in margins for error and the unexpected and therefore make it easier to meet deadlines

- how personal credibility is enhanced if work is occasionally delivered ahead of time.

It is intriguing how an ostensibly mundane activity such as setting deadlines can be a seed pod with the potential to germinate so much learning. The comforting thought is that whether you set tight or lax deadlines, or even no deadlines at all, your people will learn something from it. The only question is — is it what you want them to learn?

87 Shadowing

Shadowing is where someone observes someone else doing their job during a specific activity or period of time. Either the shadow stays mute and concentrates totally on observation and note-taking, or there is prior agreement that the shadow can ask questions and get explanations. If the shadow has intervention rights, it is important that in-flight discussions do not disrupt or alter the natural flow of events. The shadow is not there to coach, only to learn through the opportunity of being an on-the-spot observer.

There is no real substitute for first-hand observation. If someone gives you an account of what happened at, say, a meeting, it is inevitably truncated and can only be a description of his/her *perceptions* of what happened. Third party descriptions from a participant cannot possibly match, in quantity and quality, observations from a vigilant, uninvolved, on-the-spot observer.

You can easily provide your people with shadowing opportunities by giving them direct access to events that usually go on behind doors which are closed to them. Why not, for example, regularly invite different subordinates to track you through one of your normal working days? Or, if a whole day seems a bit much, for half a day or for a specific event such as a customer visit or a management meeting. Even getting a subordinate to join you while you do your in-tray (see **56**, Learning from in-trays) is better than nothing. Should something ultra sensitive or confidential crop up while you are being shadowed you can always ask the observer to withdraw while it is dealt with. You may be surprised how rarely it is necessary to do this and, if it is a concern, you can always make it a prior condition that observers respect confidences and will not blab about them afterwards (this, by the way, is an excellent way to test out which of your subordinates are really trustworthy).

If you balk at the prospect of regularly subjecting yourself to scrutiny, you could still use the shadowing idea by setting up a system where subordinates who do not normally work together shadow each other. This runs the risk of appearing like a re-hash of the old idea of 'sitting with Nellie' but there is a crucial difference. 'Sitting with Nellie' assumes that a trainee will be helped to acquire specific skills by watching someone already accomplished demonstrate those skills. (A very inefficient way, incidentally, to help anyone acquire a skill; skills can only be acquired through practise aided, preferably, by coaching and feedback.) Shadowing, on the other hand, assumes people will acquire fresh knowledge, ideas and insights from detailed observation of someone else's working habits. The skills a shadower acquires are the ones he/she is practising; observing and, if permitted, asking questions and giving feedback.

Typical lessons learned from shadowing include

- the realization that other people have different ways of doing things, some better, some worse, some just different, to your own

- fresh ideas, insights, tips and techniques on how to be more effective

- the importance of making copious notes and even noting apparently mundane events that might, in retrospect, assume a greater significance than it was possible to appreciate at the time

- how to resist the temptation to jump to conclusions and keep an open mind while gathering data (observation and interpretation do not mix)

- how to analyse notes on observations to identify themes and trends and reach considered conclusions

- how to give feedback helpfully (see 43, Giving feedback, and 70, Praising and 30, Criticizing)

Clearly, letting people observe situations they would not normally encounter provides them with valuable learning opportunities. If you are brave enough to expose yourself to scrutiny, both you and your shadow will learn concurrently and your reputation for openness and accessibility will increase dramatically (see 95, Upward appraisal/feedback).

88 Skipping levels

If you work in a hierarchical organization, even a relatively flat one, it is likely that your subordinates have little direct exposure to the upper echelons of the hierarchy. How often, for example, do your subordinates meet face-to-face with directors and board members (executive and non-executive)? If the answer to this question is hardly ever, or only on formal occasions, or only when there is a crisis, then you might like to consider the idea of instigating skip-level meetings.

Senior managers often claim to operate open door policies whereby anyone can approach them to air a grievance or propose an idea. In practice, however, the open door often proves to be more illusionary than real. Even a genuinely open door still puts the onus on the subordinate to take the initiative and be bold enough to step over the threshold. It is bold, not so much because of the reaction of the senior manager who is approached, but because of the wrath of managers in the hierarchy who have been circumvented.

Since open doors, particularly of senior managers, are rarely opened the answer is to put the process on a proper footing for all concerned. Skip-level meetings are occasions where subordinates have the opportunity to interact with senior managers who they would not normally meet. The frequency of the meetings and their structure are a matter of personal choice. Once a quarter would be admirable. The agenda is best left flexible where a senior manager says a few things about company performance, business plans and strategy, and the bulk of the meeting is given over to an off-the-record question and answer session with no holds barred. In this way subordinates get information straight from the top without the laundering and distortion that happens when messages cascade from level to level (the Chinese whispers phenomenon).

Subordinates stand to gain much from the opportunity to lock horns directly with senior managers. Some of the likely lessons learned include

-       clarification on the vision, strategy and direction in
        which the company is moving

- an understanding of how current actions are consistent, or inconsistent, with the declared strategy

- how knowing the 'big picture' has a strong, positive motivating effect on everyone (but the effect is only temporary which is one reason why a skip-level meeting should be a regular occurrence and not just a one-off)

- how most senior managers are surprisingly amenable to hard questioning and challenges (most, alas, not all)

- that nothing ventured *does* mean nothing gained (ie if you hold back and don't question, you get fobbed off with the platitudes you deserve).

If your directors and board members are out of reach and it is impossible for you to organize a skip-level meeting between all or some of them and your subordinates, you could salvage something from the idea by lowering your sights and encouraging regular sessions with your immediate boss or your boss's boss. Clearly this is unlikely to be as 'special' as a get together between more disparate hierarchical levels but it could still generate a lot of useful learning. Who knows, if you started it in a more parochial way the idea could catch on and its merits be recognized more widely.

A final point. A useful question with which to wind up a skip-level meeting is to ask the senior manager(s) what *they* have learned from the experience. Popping this question helps in a small way to put learning on the map. It also gives senior managers the chance to practise something few of them are good at; articulating what they have learned.

89 Spotting trends

Trend spotting is invariably left to specialist functions such as marketing. But it has such potential to open people's eyes and raise their awareness, that it is a shame to leave it to the experts. Discovering trends and speculating about their implications for the future is a fascinating, thought-provoking exercise and it is easy for you to encourage your people to have a dabble.

Each year the Central Statistical Office (through Her Majesty's Stationery Office) publishes a booklet called 'Social Trends'. It is packed full of information about population changes, households and families, education, employment, leisure, income and wealth, resources and expenditure, law enforcement and so on. It contains masses of information about every aspect of life in our society. In addition, there are other publications giving similar data on a global scale. Books of this genre are often to be found at discounted prices in bookshops. Newspapers too, such as the Financial Times, often do features that go into great depth on a range of different economic and sociological topics. A feast of data is therefore readily available.

All you need to do is think of an excuse to let your subordinates loose on the data and it is guaranteed that they will become absorbed and make all sorts of discoveries. It might be sufficient to pose a question such as 'what trends have, or could have, implications for our business and what should we do about them?' The more you can involve subordinates who do not normally work on cerebral exercises of this kind, the better. They stand to learn the most from the novelty of spotting trends and thinking through implications. It is also possible that the unfamiliarity of the task will make it more, not less, likely that they will come up with something fresh; an interesting connection that the experts might have overlooked.

You might also consider posing your question the other way round; 'what trends do not have implications for our business and why not?' This helps to ensure that data that would be dismissed as irrelevant comes under scrutiny, if only to prove that they shouldn't.

Trend spotting will help your subordinates learn how to

- absorb and process large amounts of detailed data

- make fresh connections and identify trends and themes that were not necessarily apparent at first sight

- think through implications and consequences (see 6, Anticipating consequences)

- generate ideas and recommendations for courses of action and persuasive arguments to support them.

As a spin-off your subordinates will also become extraordinarily well informed about national and international affairs with statistics of the 'not many people know this' variety at their finger tips. And with any luck they'll come up with some useful ideas to advance the business.

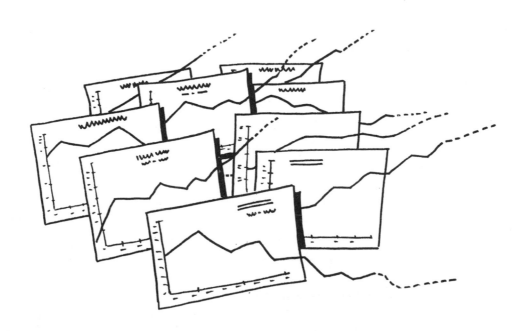

90 Stress management

Stress is always subjective; an emotional reaction to outside events. Certain levels of stress are helpful and enhance people's performance but everyone has a point where enough is enough and too much stress has an adverse effect. Potential stressors at work are many and varied. Frequently cited are

- ambiguity and uncertainty
- bureaucracy
- conflicting priorities
- criticism and negative feedback
- impossible deadlines/overdemanding tasks
- disagreements, power struggles and 'personality clashes'
- interruptions
- mistakes
- travelling
- not having enough to do/waiting.

It is inevitable that from time to time your people will feel stressed to the point where their performance is impaired and, even though this is an unpleasant experience, stress is a trigger for learning and development. When people feel stressed they are not complacent, and complacency is the biggest single enemy to continuous improvement and development. Stressed people want to learn how to alleviate the stress they are feeling now, and prevent it in the future.

Because stress is an emotion that is 'owned' by the stressed person, you have to be careful to be helpful but to leave him/her with the responsibility to take action. It is tempting, but ultimately unhelpful, to take it upon yourself to solve the other person's problem. To do so would be futile and would deprive the stressed person of a tough but invaluable learning opportunity.

There are two lines of exploration you can take to help a stressed person solve their own problem and learn from the experience.

1.   Get the stressed person to identify the stressors, ie the things that happen that trigger their feelings of stress. Stressors might be anything from spiders to the photocopying machine breaking down at a critical time.

When they have identified the things that trigger their stress, ask them for ideas on what action they can take to improve the situation. Wait for them to come up with an idea before you offer any suggestions yourself. This shows that you are expecting them to solve their own problem, not you to work some impossible miracle.

2.	Explore with the stressed person what they think about the situation that triggers their stress. The chances are that they are exaggerating the awfulness of the situation and being too dogmatic about what should happen. The greater the gap they perceive between what *is* happening and what they believe *should* happen the more frustrated and stressed they are likely to feel. As the exaggerations and dogma surface, help the stressed person to see how their unrealistic thoughts are the key to understanding why they are stressed. If the stressed person can accept that it is their own thoughts and perceptions that make them feel stressed, and not the situation itself, you will have helped them learn an invaluable lesson.

There are some profound lessons to learn from the experience of being stressed amongst them being

-	external events, however unfortunate, cannot by themselves *make* me stressed; it is what I think about the events that causes the stress. ('There is nothing good nor bad, but thinking makes it so' Shakespeare)

-	I can choose how I feel in the same way that I can choose how I behave

-	the thoughts that do the damage and cause me to feel stressed exaggerate the seriousness of the situation ('it would be Awful, Catastrophic, Terrible, Intolerable if...') and make unrealistic, dogmatic demands (shoulds, oughts and musts)

-	I am less vulnerable to feeling stressed if I make my thoughts more realistic, ie close the gap by reducing the exaggerations and the dogmatic imperatives

-     I, and I alone, am responsible for my feelings and emotions. No-one else is to blame and no-one else can stop me feeling stressed.

Whilst feelings of stress are never welcome, they create opportunities to learn and develop. You can help your subordinates to gain from the pain.

91 Surfacing expectations

Everyone has expectations; some realistic, some unrealistic. Your subordinates have expectations of you as their boss in just the same way that you have expectations of them. An interesting feature of expectations is that they markedly affect people's perceptions. If expectations are low, then it is easy to exceed them. If expectations are high, it is difficult to meet them, let alone exceed them. Anything you can do, therefore, to get your subordinates to have realistic expectations will help them to feel satisfied more often than dissatisfied.

Whilst everyone has expectations of this, that and the other, they invariably operate at a tacit, unspoken level. Surfacing expectations so that they can be shared, explored and checked for realism is not only a useful exercise in its own right, but also a learning experience for all concerned.

It isn't easy for people to articulate things that operate at a subliminal level, but it is relatively easy for you to start the ball rolling. It can be as simple as remembering to ask people what they expect of

- people, such as customers, colleagues, subordinates, bosses

- events, such as a customer visit, a management meeting, a training course, a product launch, a budget review, a video conference

- services, such as those provided by a hotel, a restaurant, a garage, an airline

- places and things, such as an open plan office, a new computer system, a new photocopier or other piece of office equipment.

A good way to start would be to ask each of your subordinates to produce a written list describing their expectations of you, their boss, and to categorize each as either 'essential' or 'desirable'. No-one would trouble to undertake such an irksome task unless it was in response to a specific request but, having gone through the process, most people will admit it was useful. Making explicit things that are normally tacit and 'holding them up to the light' always generates insights which would otherwise have lain undiscovered.

From your point of view, the expectations once surfaced make fascinating reading and may contain some surprises. They could be the starting point for a role clarification exercise where you commit yourself to meet certain expectations and explain why you cannot, or will not, subscribe to others. Clearing the air in this way reduces misunderstandings.

Surfacing expectations helps your subordinates to learn the considerable part expectations play in shaping people's perceptions and the value of bringing such a key player 'out of the closet'. They will also discover that expectations are adjustable, up or down, but only after they have been made explicit. Your subordinates might even lower their expectations of you to the point where you can't help but exceed them. Reduce expectations to avoid disappointment!

92 Teamwork

Working in groups or teams (a team is a group but a group is not necessarily a team) has always been an important contributor to effectiveness and productivity. Recent changes in many organizations have tended to make teamwork even more important than it has always been. For example

- the flattening of hierarchical levels (the traditional 'pyramid') means people have to be more interdependent in order to achieve more with less

- the whole quest for Total Quality, continuous improvement and improved customer service means that functional barriers are breached and people 'forced' to cooperate *between* functions, not just within a function

- the need to respond more rapidly to market forces, and changes external to the organization, means that organization structures are more complex (matrix management is just one example) and more flexible. This increases the need for collaborative decision making (more 'we' decisions less 'I' decisions)

- raised expectations about participating in, or at the very least being consulted about, decisions that affect people and their work practices. This automatically increases the demand for more group/team decision making

- the increased use of project teams and task forces, often multi-disciplinary, to come together rapidly to tackle a major issue or problem and then disband

- the empowerment movement and the changing role of managers, from 'command and control' to enabling and empowering, inevitably puts greater emphasis on the group/team and less on 'divide-and-conquer' management styles

- last but not least, the attempts (albeit patchy) to create learning organizations. This is only possible if teams meet frequently to trawl their experiences for learning and agree what to do better/differently in future. The key to creating a learning organization is to have lots of overlapping learning teams.

Despite the ground swell toward teamwork, for many people working in groups or teams is a frustrating, even exasperating, experience. The struggle to cohere and produce something that is more than the sum of the individual parts is beyond the experience and comprehension of individualists and mavericks. They fear (and sometimes they are right) that group work is convoluted and results in compromises in the worst sense of the word. But even when a group or team fails to produce the goods, the experience is rich in learning opportunities. Just consider the following list of potential lessons learned

- the naivety of assuming that all team members share a common understanding of the objective and terms of reference and that time invested in testing understanding is time well spent

- the temptation to become task mesmerized to the detriment of process considerations, ie a plan to get from here to there, an agreed *modus operandi*, behaviours that help, behaviours that hinder

- how teams thrive on the differences between its members, not the similarities. The greater the differences in background, skills and functions, the greater the potential for synergy

- how the style of the team leader needs to change depending on the circumstances; when things are chaotic tending to be directive and when things are going smoothly and according to plan tending to be non-directive

- how small pieces of behaviour make all the difference in determining whether the working atmosphere is tense and competitive or relaxed and co-operative. For example, the ratio of supportive comments to critical comments, whether ideas are developed or dismissed, whether people listen or

interrupt

-   how teams have to learn to walk together before they can run, ie to work at a formal level and err on the side of having explicit disciplines *before* it is safe to relax and cut corners without jeopardizing the team's effectiveness

-   how it is vital to allocate time for process/learning reviews where team members share their perceptions of what went well and what could have gone better and agree a plan to improve the team's performance next time they work together.

Teamwork is undoubtedly the most appropriate way to accomplish certain tasks and, *at the same time*, is a powerful generator of learning and developmental opportunities. If it is possible to rotate the role of leader so that over the team's existence different people get to have a go, this further increases learning opportunities. Individuals learn from being in the hot seat; the team learns from being able to contrast different styles and discover their effects, for better or worse, on the team's performance.

From a learning point of view, teams are unquestionably 'a Good Thing'.

93 Testing understanding

Testing understanding, or paraphrasing, is a specific technique to check that people have heard and understood what someone has said. Listening is a skill which people assume they already do well. Most people, however, only do part of what is involved. Effective listening follows a three step sequence

1   You hear what is said
2   You understand what you heard
3   You interpret what you understood

only then is it safe to respond. The main hazard is to do half of number 1, leapfrog number 2 and jump to number 3. Testing understanding forces people to hear and understand *before* they interpret.

Testing understanding can either be imposed or undertaken voluntarily. If you impose it you simply invite a named person to paraphrase, in his/her own words, the essence of what the listener has heard. This automatically checks understanding, makes it more likely that the interpretation will be correct and gives the speaker an early opportunity to correct any misunderstandings. If all the listeners know in advance that paraphrases are going to be demanded from time to time, it works wonders for effective listening. No-one wants to be caught out with an inadequate paraphrase and exposed as a poor listener.

Alternatively, any listener, at any time, can offer to paraphrase. Voluntary paraphrasing is one of the hallmarks of an interactively skilled person.

Paraphrasing, whether imposed or volunteered, massively ups the learning stakes because listening, along with reading, is a major information conduit. Listening is the way to acquire more ideas, facts and opinions than would otherwise be possible.

It is easy for you to start the ball rolling by testing if you have understood what other people say to you or by inviting your listeners to paraphrase what you say to them. You can make paraphrasing the rule, rather than the exception, in all meetings and discussions. Testing understanding is a small technique with a big payoff.

94 Training videos

There are many excellent training videos available for purchase or hire. Typically a video lasts twenty minutes or so and is always accompanied with a useful booklet expanding on the subject matter and giving ideas on how to incorporate the video into a mini-training session. Every subject under the sun is available from finance for non-financial personnel to assertiveness and customer care.

Obviously training videos are designed to put certain messages across and are therefore tailor-made for learning. But watching a video is an essentially passive activity (technology is in the process of putting this right with the advent of interactive multimedia techniques) and with a little thought you can make it more purposeful and enhance the learning. For example you can

- devise a quiz to see how much people know before and after watching the video

- get people to discuss the video as if they were film critics

- after watching the video have a short debate on a contentious aspect

- get people to work out the implications for their work practices of the messages the video put across

- get people to commit themselves to at least one action to improve performance in the light of the video's messages.

If you find the prospect of organizing mini-training sessions using videos daunting, then delegate it. You could put a different person in charge of masterminding the whole thing at, say, monthly sessions. Make it a rule that each session lasts for a maximum of seventy-five minutes including preliminaries, the video itself and the ensuing discussion. If you want to save time, get people to view the video in their own time and then come together for a forty-five minute discussion on lessons learned.

To get full value out of training videos it is vital to regard them as catalysts for learning rather than ends in themselves. However good the video, what matters is the translation of its generic messages into specific actions that are relevant to your circumstances.

95 Upward appraisal/feedback

The more you consult your subordinates the more you enrich their experiences and, as a consequence, their opportunities to learn. Perhaps the most potent consultation of all is where you solicit feedback from your subordinates about your performance as their manager.

Upward appraisal and feedback are often talked about but rarely done. By inviting feedback from your subordinates you and they stand to learn and, in addition, you send out an important message about feedback and your own preparedness to learn from it yourself.

Rather than demanding off-the-cuff feedback, it is best to organize things so that your subordinates can give the matter proper consideration. You might have to start by contenting yourself with anonymous feedback until you have created a climate where people are prepared to be totally open and honest. You could use a checklist of competencies (see 96, Using competencies) and get your subordinates to rate you against them using a simple four point scale such as very good, good, could be better, poor. Always leave plenty of space for comments and examples and encourage people to expand on their ticks in boxes.

If you want to establish how your subordinates rate you when it comes to helping with their development, try using a short checklist of paired statements like this

My boss

1 A ☐ Helps me to analyse my strengths and weaknesses

B ☐ Never talks over my strengths and weaknesses

2 A ☐ Encourages me to 'have a go' and take a risk for develop-ment purposes

B ☐ Discourages me from taking risks involved in trying some-thing new or different

3 A ☐	Gives time to reviewing and appraising my performance	B ☐	Only reviews my performance once a year as part of the formal system

4 A ☐	Involves me in some of his/her important tasks	B ☐	Only delegates 'Micky Mouse' tasks to me

5 A ☐	Shares some of his/her problems and anxieties with me	B ☐	Is not open about his/her problems and anxieties

6 A ☐	Listens rather than talks	B ☐	Talks rather than listens

7 A ☐	Gives me helpful feedback/ coaching with constructive suggestions	B ☐	Avoids giving me feedback/coaching or does so in a clinical, negative way

Clearly the more 'A' statements that are ticked the rosier the feedback.

The whole idea of using anonymous checklists is to establish a precedent and get your subordinates used to the idea of upward feedback. You need to progress to a stage where they are happy to put their names to the feedback and, eventually, to a stage where they are comfortable with giving you candid feedback face-to-face.

Your behaviour in response to the feedback determines the success or otherwise of the whole venture. The answer is to stay in learning mode and only permit yourself to ask questions of clarification. Defensive explanations are out, as is anything that could be construed as 'shooting the messenger'. It is easier not to take umbrage, even with feedback you consider ignorant or unfair, if you remember that it isn't feedback about you the whole person; merely about some aspect of your behaviour. Separating the person from the person's outward actions is a useful skill both when giving and receiving feedback.

It also helps to remember that you, the receiver of feedback, are always the final arbiter. You, and you alone, have to decide whether to accept the feedback and act on it or whether to reject the feedback. It's *always* your choice.

96 Using competencies

Competencies are much in vogue at present. Many organizations have conducted research in a variety of different ways to pinpoint the skills, behaviours and attributes people require in order to perform a given job competently. A number of national initiatives, such as Investors in People, the Management Charter Initiative (MCI), National Vocational Qualifications (NVQs) and Citizen's Charters, have all been inspired by the competencies movement.

Competencies describe characteristics that can be measured, or counted reliably, which differentiate significantly between superior and average performers or between effective and ineffective performers. Some competencies are deemed to be essential for effective performance while others describe the thresholds necessary for average performance.

People and jobs vary and so, inevitably, the competencies that are relevant will also vary. However it appears from numerous research studies that there are some 'core' competencies that crop up again and again and are sufficiently generic to apply to a broad cross section of people and jobs. The thirteen personal effectiveness competencies used by the Management Charter Initiative are but one example amongst many.

> Showing concern for excellence
> Setting and prioritising objectives
> Monitoring and responding to actual against planned activities
> Showing sensitivity to the needs of others
> Relating to others
> Obtaining the commitment of others
> Presenting oneself positively to others
> Showing self-confidence and personal drive
> Managing personal emotions and stress
> Managing personal learning and development
> Collecting and organizing information
> Identifying and applying concepts
> Taking decisions

Each competency is then broken down into a number of specific behavioural indicators; eighty in the case of the MCI competencies.

There are a number of possibilities when it comes to using competencies to help your people develop. They fall into two categories; helping your subordinates to

- identify which competencies are important in their current job

- decide which competencies to develop (strengths or weaknesses or a mixture of both).

You could get hold of a checklist of generic competencies and ask each of your subordinates to indicate which competencies he/she

- perceives as being most important for their effectiveness in their current job

- needs to get better at. Use a simple rating system such as

  1 - a very important development need
  2 - a moderately important development need
  3 - not a development need.

You can assess subordinates using the same checklist of competencies and then compare your perceptions with theirs. Where you have big discrepancies, talk them through. There is much to learn from understanding the reasons why someone has reached a different conclusion to your own and *vice versa*. Suppose, for example, you have assessed the competency 'relating to others' as very important, both for effectiveness in the job and as a development need for the person, and your subordinate does not rate it as important on either count, then you have a golden opportunity to explore and resolve this difference. At the very least your subordinate will become clearer about your expectations and, hopefully, you will be able to convince him/her to give 'relating to others' a higher priority than hitherto.

If you want to do a more thorough assessment, get your subordinates to canvas other people's views by getting, say, a colleague or two or a customer or a subordinate to complete the checklist. Then look for trends, similarities and differences in the assessments.

Once you have agreed on some development needs, one, two or three maximum will suffice, you need to help your subordinates to produce personal development plans to meet the identified needs (see 69, Planning). The best plans are simple and linked to opportunities that are likely to crop up in the near future. It is preferable to identify an opportunity before planning how to use it. This book should provide you with plenty of thought starters about how to identify everyday opportunities to which development can be coupled.

Competencies are an excellent starting point for development and, of course, you can always repeat the exercise to update assessments and get a 'before and after' feel for progress.

97 Using SWOT

SWOT is an analytical technique that helps people think strategically. The letters are a mnemonic standing for Strengths, Weaknesses, Opportunities and Threats. The technique works by forcing people to give good news and bad news equal consideration. It thus helps people who are inclined to be pessimistic to be more optimistic and optimists to be realists. The whole technique depends, as so many do, on stimulating thought by setting up contrasts between strengths and weaknesses and between opportunities and threats. It is the juxtaposition of these extremes that does the trick (see 100, Weighing up pros and cons).

The SWOT technique is usually used to explore the strategic position of a product or business but it can equally well be used by individuals to help them take stock of their strengths and weaknesses and work out a development strategy. At its simplest (there is much more to the technique than this), you merely need to pose four questions

-   what are your strengths, ie the things you are good at?

-   what are your weaknesses, ie the things you are bad at?

-   what opportunities do you seek for yourself, ie opportunities you can take and opportunities you can make?

-   what threats do you see, ie things that could, or might, jeopardize the opportunities you seek?

Despite the mnemonic, these questions do not have to be answered in this order. It is often better for example to start with opportunities (see 82, Searching for opportunities) then to temper them by identifying the threats to those opportunities. Once opportunities have been realistically assessed, strengths and weaknesses can be introduced with plans to use the opportunities to build on strengths and/or overcome weaknesses. It is infinitely preferable to have an opportunity in search of a plan to exploit it rather than a plan in search of an opportunity to implement it.

The SWOT technique provides a useful framework, or discipline. It is not designed to generate ready-made strategies; only to pave the way by encouraging rigorous examination of the basic ingredients.

Using SWOT not only helps to produce sound, implementable strategies, it also is a learning experience in its own right. The process abounds in opportunities to think, analyse, make judgements and evaluate. If Rodin's famous statue 'The Thinker' had used the SWOT technique perhaps it would appear less pensive!

If you want to know much more about SWOT, the definitive text is 'Dynamic SWOT Analysis' by T.R. Dealtry published by Dynamic SWOT Associates, Birmingham. Telephone 021-427-6949

98 Using training programmes

Contrived off-the-job learning experiences, such as courses, workshops, conferences and seminars, obviously have an important contribution to make to learning and development. Designed properly, they provide a focused, safe environment, free from distractions, where learning is the undisputed purpose. But, and this is a big but, people are able to spend but a fraction of their time attending courses. More than ninety percent of their time is spent at their place of work. This is precisely why work-based learning has much more to offer than any course ever can.

There is another reason why work-based learning wins hands down. The Achilles heel with off-the-job training programmes is how to transfer what has been learned on the course to the work place where the people, priorities and pressures are quite different. The design of the course might have been exemplary but when it ends, as end it must, each person is left with the biggest problem of all; how to apply what has been learned in an 'artificial' situation to the real world. It is the equivalent of the problems the space shuttle encounters whenever it re-enters the earth's atmosphere. Special heat absorbing tiles ensure that it doesn't get burnt up. Each person returning from a course needs similar protection to ensure they survive the perils of re-entry.

What happens before and what happens after a course is a far more important determinant of lasting learning and development than anything that happens during the course (and this is not to belittle the importance of the 'durings'). It follows, therefore, that you, the manager, hold the key to success since you have most influence over the all-important 'befores' and 'afters'. Here is a list to help you pinpoint exactly what to do to ensure the success of off-the-job training programmes for your people.

Activity	Prime Responsibility
Before the training programme	
1. Setting objectives and reviewing people's performance against them.	Manager

2.	Providing trainers with information about current and future performance problems.	Manager
3.	Keeping in touch with the business and identifying training needs.	Trainer
4.	Checking that trainers have correctly identified the needs.	Manager
5.	Converting needs into training objectives.	Trainer
6.	Checking that trainers have set the right objectives.	Manager
7.	Deciding on methods/resources to meet the need.	Trainer
8.	Designing learning opportunities and producing training materials (or contracting this out to those who have the expertise).	Trainer
9.	Briefing learners prior to undertaking training and helping them to set learning objectives.	Manager
10.	Understanding the learning opportunity and setting appropriate learning objectives.	Learner

During the training programme

11.	Helping people learn by providing learning opportunities backed by feedback, guidance and instruction (or contracting this out to those who have the expertise).	Trainer
12.	Seizing learning opportunities (having a go, experimenting, questioning, etc.).	Learner
13.	Checking that the training objectives have been achieved (validation).	Trainer

After the training programme

14.	Debriefing learners after undertaking the training and helping them plan implementation.	Manager
15.	Implementing what has been learned and soliciting assistance from his/her manager.	Learner
16.	Providing learners with adequate opportunities to implement what they have learned with encouragement and feedback.	Manager
17.	Providing follow-up activities to help managers and learners with implementation.	Trainer
18.	Checking that the training succeeded in improving job performance (evaluation).	Manager
19.	Giving trainers feedback about the success or otherwise of the training.	Manager
20.	Improving and updating the training methods and materials (or, if the training has been contracted out, ensuring this is done by those who have the expertise).	Trainer

This list shows that even when you use training programmes to aid development, where it would be tempting to assume the trainer has responsibility for most aspects, you, the manager, retain prime responsibility for nearly fifty percent of the activities; all of them either before or after the delivery of the training.

If you find the list daunting and want to whittle down your responsibilities then the following four are absolute musts.

- Setting objectives and reviewing people's performance against them (item 1).

- Briefing learners prior to undertaking training and helping them to set learning objectives (item 9).

- Debriefing learners after undertaking the training and helping them to plan implementation (item **14**).

- Providing learners with adequate opportunities to supplement what they have learned with encouragement and feedback (item **16**).

Even when you use off-the-job training programmes, you remain a key factor in determining whether it has all been worthwhile.

99 Visioning

A vision is an expression of a preferred future. It describes an ideal that you passionately want to reach. Since the vision is an ideal, you will never reach it; but it gives you something worthwhile to pursue, a lofty ideal that gives consistency and purpose to your actions and helps you manage the present from the future.

The distinction between a *predicted* and a *preferred* future is vital. A predicted future is merely a prediction of what is likely to happen based on past experience. It is an extension of what has happened in the past. Goals, objectives and targets all fall into this category; they are heavily contaminated with judgements about what is possible based on past trends. Of course, quite often something unexpected happens and the prediction is proved wrong but all predictions are based on the assumption that the future will be little different from the past.

A preferred future is quite different. A preferred future is unencumbered by constraints, restrictions and practicalities. It is a conceptual leap that breaks free of existing paradigms about what is likely or possible. It is an unqualified expression of what you very much want. Vision is seeing the masterpiece while you mix the paints.

Most people find it difficult to give themselves permission to indulge in some visioning. They would prefer to stay safe and take a predictable path. Or they would prefer someone else to generate the vision and pay lip service to that. To do so is perhaps the ultimate cop out; a vote for compliance and dependency and against autonomy and empowerment.

Creating a vision, a picture of a preferred future, is not something you can demand of people; 'Have your vision on my desk first thing in the morning'. There are, however, things you can do to facilitate the creation and expression of a vision by your people. You could start by having a vision for your department or unit and making it clear to your subordinates. You would do this not to sell them your vision but to encourage them to dream also and express their own visions. Your vision, unlike objectives, will sound like 'motherhood and apple pie' because it is an expression of an unattainable dream which nonetheless sets standards for your behaviour and actions. Examples of visions are

- expectations that are exceeded (not just met)
- subordinates who are king
- synergy in every meeting
- customers who are not satisfied; they are delighted
- life long learning
- zero defects
- everyone takes responsibility for their own actions
- every encounter adds value
- a blame free culture
- rules that are handrails, not handcuffs.

Another major contribution to enabling your people to create their own preferred futures is to encourage them to talk about their visions. This needn't be as daunting as it sounds if you ease people into it with a question such as 'what is your picture of an ideal service/product/meeting/boss/organization/customer?' Don't expect a ready-made, pat answer. It may take a number of repetitions before the right words are found to express the vision succinctly.

Your subordinates stand to learn a number of profound lessons from the struggle to articulate an inspirational vision. For example

- the difference between pedestrian predictions of the future, ie extensions of the past, and preferred futures, ie impossible ideals

- how a vision gives purpose and consistency to current actions, ie it is the journey that is important, not reaching the destination

- how everyone has a vision even if it has not been made explicit or put into words

- how even though visions are non-negotiable, it helps to know the vision of the people we work with and for

- how a clear vision is the key to taking responsibility for our own actions; to constructive autonomy.

You need to help people to come out of the closet and express their visions. To do so not only generates learning, it is also an essential step towards empowerment. For inspiration read 'The Empowered Manager' by Peter Block, published by Jossey-Bass, ISBN 1-55542-265-9.

100   Weighing up pros and cons

People who identify options and weigh up the pros and cons of each are far more likely to make sound decisions than people who seize on the first expedient course of action. Unfortunately many people, when faced with a problem, have a compulsion to find a quick solution either because they have a low tolerance for unresolved problems or for ambiguity or both.

You can help people to become better problem solvers and acquire an essential learning skill by insisting on the identification and analysis of at least three options before a decision is taken. This discipline forces people to do a number of worthwhile things such as

- search for at least three possible courses of action

- draw up a list of advantages for each course of action

- draw up a list of disadvantages for each course of action

- decide what criteria to use to weigh up the advantages and disadvantages (ie practicality, feasibility, acceptability, cost effectiveness)

- apply the criteria and make a decision on the best course of action

- convince others that the chosen course of action is, all things considered, the best.

In addition, the existence of explicit criteria upon which the decision is based makes it easier to monitor and evaluate the effectiveness of the chosen course of action once it has been implemented.

If you insist on the three options discipline, you will help your subordinates learn some important lessons, amongst them being

- it is never true to say 'there is no alternative'; there is *always* a choice

- even intuitive 'gut feel' decisions should be checked out to see how they compare with other options (sometimes the intuitive decision will be confirmed as the best, sometimes it won't)

- it isn't only the sheer number of advantages/ disadvantages that win the day, more important is the weight each carries against the criteria

- it is easier to make a convincing case for a course of action if alternatives can be cited and shown to be wanting (see **65**, Persuading and influencing).

Your insistence on three options will force your subordinates to become better problem-solvers and decision-makers and, at the same time, increase their learning and development. Three outcomes all from one insistence.

101 Writing

Writing isn't as frequent an activity for many people as talking or reading but nonetheless it has a useful contribution to make to the learning process. The act of expressing something clearly and succinctly *in writing* forces the writer to clarify his/her thoughts. Talking has much the same effect but writing is a slower more laborious process and as a consequence tends to stimulate deeper reflection. Also, writing is more of a commitment than talking. Records can more easily be kept and subsequently something in writing can act as a reminder (or return to haunt you!).

Iacocca summed it up perfectly in his autobiography when he said 'The discipline of writing something down is the first step towards making it happen. In conversation you can get away with all kinds of vagueness and nonsense, often without even realizing it. But there's something about putting your thoughts on paper that forces you to get down to specifics. That way it's harder to deceive yourself or anybody else'.

Insisting that people put their thoughts on paper automatically increases learning. It may seem an unnecessary chore, and people will try to wriggle out of it, but there is no doubt that writing adds value. In an obtuse sort of way, the people who are most resistant and least fluent stand to gain most as they struggle to express themselves on paper.

There are numerous small opportunities to get people to write. Whenever, for example, someone enthuses about an idea, ask them to put it down on one side of A4 (see 73, Producing one-pagers). You could invite people to meetings as minute takers. You could empower people to write letters and memos.

Bigger opportunities can also be engineered by getting your subordinates to write reports. Even more ambitiously, you could invite them to write pieces for the company magazine or for external trade journals. If there is advertising or marketing copy to produce, get your subordinates to have a stab at it before it goes to an agency.

Best of all, get your subordinates to write learning logs (see 54, Keeping learning logs) and/or keep notes on their experiences and what they have learned from them. This immediately results in a double value pay-off; your subordinates develop their writing skills and simultaneously convert tacit learning into something more explicit.

It helps to get people into the swing of things if you encourage them to write, write, write, in an uncensored, unstructured, spontaneous way then to reflect and edit afterwards. Make it clear that literary correctness, spelling and grammar are secondary considerations. Eloquence and succinctness will come. The first hurdle is to overcome procrastination and fear of the blank page, and get something down. The idea is to write in order to crystallize and clarify, not to win the Booker prize.

Other publications available direct from Peter Honey

THE MANUAL OF LEARNING STYLES

This has sold thousands of copies worldwide since the first edition was published in 1982. The Manual includes

*   descriptions of the Learning Cycle and four styles - Activist, Reflector, Theorist and Pragmatist

*   the Learning Styles Questionnaire which enables people to identify their preferred style(s)

*   a variety of norms against which results can be compared

*   suggestions on how trainers can use the information to

    -       design events to cover the complete learning cycle
    -       select activities to suit different preferences
    -       help individuals to build on learning strengths and reduce weaknesses

*   suggestions on how people can better manage their learning.

Each Manual comes complete with a master copy of the questionnaire and score key, both of which can be photocopied.

USING YOUR LEARNING STYLES

This is a personal workbook for an individual learner and makes an excellent handout for people who have completed the Learning Styles Questionnaire.

The booklet offers help on

*   understanding the questionnaire result
*   choosing activities to suit learning style preferences
*   making best use of learning strengths
*   expanding the repertoire of learning styles
*   getting help from others including bosses and colleagues.

Dr Alan Mumford is the co-author of both these publications.

THE MANUAL OF LEARNING OPPORTUNITIES

A loose-leaf binder full of questionnaires, check lists and exercises to help people become better at making and taking learning opportunities in the normal course of their work. The most potent tool is the Learning Diagnostic Questionnaire which analyses the factors that combine together to create ideal conditions for learning, namely

* the knowledge and skills to learn from a variety of experiences

* a working situation that provides ample learning opportunities and encouragement

* positive attitudes and emotions about learning

In addition the Manual contains over thirty exercises, all of which can be photocopied, with advice on

- learning processes and skills
- incremental opportunities for learning
- transformational opportunities for learning.

THE OPPORTUNIST LEARNER

This guide is full of ideas to help the individual learner become more effective. It builds on the material in 'The Manual of Learning Opportunities' with 23 further exercises and suggestions for action at work and on courses. The guide can be used as a handout or as a self directed/distance learning resource. It gives guidance on how to

* improve recognition and use of learning opportunities

* tackle the issues revealed by answers to the Learning Diagnostic Questionnaire

* improve learning methods and approaches.

Dr Alan Mumford is the co-author of both these publications.

PETER HONEY'S MANUAL OF SELF-ASSESSMENT QUESTIONNAIRES

A loose-leaf binder containing twenty-one questionnaires, score keys and supporting documentation. The questionnaires are published in eight sections as follows

Section 1: ASSERTIVENESS

Assertiveness Beliefs Check
Face to Face Assertiveness
Telephone Assertiveness

Section 2: ATTITUDES AND EMOTIONS

Optimist - Pessimist Questionnaire
How Good are You at Managing Your Emotions?
Taking Charge of Your Temper
Values Questionnaire

Section 3: BEHAVIOUR STYLES

Interpersonal Skills Questionnaire
Influencing Styles Questionnaire
Win - Win Questionnaire
Counselling Styles Questionnaire

Section 4: CREATIVE THINKING

Creative Thinking Questionnaire
Left Brain - Right Brain Questionnaire

Section 5: LEARNING AND SELF-DEVELOPMENT

Self-Development Beliefs Check
Are You an Effective Learner from Experience?
Learning Organization Questionnaire

Section 6: SOLVING PEOPLE-PROBLEMS

Are you a Good Solver of People-Problems?
Performance Improvement Questionnaire

Section 7: TEAMWORK

Teamwork Check
Team Roles Questionnaire

Section 8: TRAINER COMPETENCE

Trainer Competence Questionnaire

A final section gives step-by-step advice on how trainers can devise their own self-assessment questionnaires and check reliability and validity and calculate norms.

PETER HONEY'S MANUAL OF MANAGEMENT WORKSHOPS

What exactly is a workshop?
What are the advantages of a workshop?
What do you do before and after a workshop to make it a success?
How do you decide what tasks to build into a workshop?
How do you get a balance between 'doing' and 'learning'?

All these questions, and many more, are answered in this Manual. It contains full details of three of Peter Honey's management workshops, each of which has evolved over a ten year period and been run many times both in-company and as 'open' events. The Manual includes *all* the documentation, handouts, task briefs, etc., for each workshop with Peter Honey's permission to reproduce any or all of it for your own use.

The three workshops in this Manual are

-       a 2-day **learning/self-development workshop**, with **24** handouts, designed to help managers become better learners from experience

-       a 3-day **'process' workshop**, with **31** handouts, designed to develop the skills of helping groups and teams to function more skilfully

-       a 2-day **solving people-problems workshop**, with **27** handouts, designed to help managers to analyse and solve problems with other people themselves.

IMPROVE YOUR PEOPLE SKILLS
Published by the Institute of Personnel Management

This book is written in 122 short alphabetical sections and shows how to do virtually everything from participating in meetings to being assertive to being persuasive. The book is a mini-encyclopedia of different techniques and approaches for handling people.

Examples of contents: Asking questions; Attitudes; Beliefs; Brainstorming; Chairing meetings; Conflict; Delegation; Disagreeing; Ego-states; Empathy; Feedback; Feelings; Games; Groups; Habits; Humour; Interpersonal skills; Interviewing; Leadership; Learning from experience; Manipulation...and 100 more entries.

FACE TO FACE SKILLS
Published by Gower

Most people spend a large part of their time in face-to-face encounters of one kind or another. This includes formal occasions such as meetings and presentations, and less formal interactions involving two or more people. The book shows how people tend to repeat behaviour patterns because of their familiarity rather than because they are appropriate or effective. This book offers a way of identifying and classifying behaviour and shows how to harness both spoken and non-verbal behaviour to help you achieve your objectives.

Contents: Introducing behaviour; Situations, objectives and behaviour; Exercises in behaviour recognition; Developing realistic objectives; How to analyse behaviour; Exercises in behaviour analysis; How to shape other people's behaviour; Non-verbal behaviour; How to plan behaviour; What is interactive competence?

PROBLEM PEOPLE AND HOW TO MANAGE THEM
Published by the Institute of Personnel Management

This book focuses on people who persist in behaving in ways that create problems for you. It features 50 problem-people in short sections that explore four options: the pros and cons of doing nothing, ways to alter your perception of the problem, the possibility of persuading the problem-person to change and modifying the behaviour by changing the situation.

Contents: Introducing problem-people and people problems; Are you a good problem owner/solver?; Problem-people: the options; Abdicator, Absentee; Apathetic; Arrogant; Authoritarian; Boaster; Bolshie; Bore; Buck-Passer; Bureaucrat; Circuitous; Coaster; Conservative; Defensive; Ditherer; Dogmatic; Eccentric; Flippant; Gamesman; Gossip; Humourless; Impulsive; Intimidator; Judgemental; Kowtower; Lazy; Manipulator; Martyr; Meddler; Nagger; Overpowering; Perfectionist; Pessimist; Plagiarist; Prejudiced; Procrastinator; Quarrelsome; Reserved; Sarcastic; Scatterbrained; Secretive; Self-conscious; Slapdash; Tactless; Temperamental; Two-faced; Vague; Whinger; Workaholic; Worrier.

SOLVING PEOPLE-PROBLEMS
Published by McGraw-Hill

This book shows you how you can solve those people-problems you thought you simply had to endure. It gives positive, practical guidelines for dealing with uncooperative people, lazy people, negative people - and the people (bosses included) with whom you have personality clashes. The book suggests how to prevent people-problems and explains why they are so prevalent in most organizations.

Contents: What are people-problems? Traditional ways of tackling people-problems; A new approach to solving people-problems; Solving people-problems successfully; Why people-problems are so prevalent; The new approach and the management of people; Some background theory and basic principles; Limitations and objections; Exercises for solving people-problems; How to modify your own unwanted behaviour and feelings.

THE LEARNING EXPERIENCE
Published by BBC Training Videos

A twenty-five minute video introducing the learning cycle and learning styles together with an eighty page booklet. The video features some Ford managers on an executive development programme, each with different learning style preferences. The impact of their styles both for their behaviour on the programme and back at work are explored.

The contents of the booklet are

The Learning Experience: introduction to the video; Introduction to Learning from Experience; The Learning Cycle; Learning Styles; How to Strengthen Under-utilized Styles; Solo Learning: How to Keep a Learning Log; Group Learning: How to Conduct a Learning Review; Becoming a Learning Opportunist; Creating a Learning Organization; A one day 'Learning to Learn' workshop; Handouts; Further Reading; The Iterative Secret.